STARESHA LEE

Grace in Her Wounds

Dedication

For my three beautiful children—
You have seen me break and watched me rise.
You are my reason, my reminder, and my greatest gift.
Every chapter of my healing carries your names;
May you always know the power of grace
and the beauty of beginning again.

"But he said to me, "My grace is sufficient for you, for my power is made perfect in weakness." Therefore I will boast all the more gladly of my weaknesses, so that the power of Christ may rest upon me"

2 Corinthians 12:9

Contents

Introduction

My life has never been a straight line. It's been a mix of sweetness and heartbreak, joy and confusion, love and loss—woven together in a way that only God could make sense of. When I look back over my journey, I see the fingerprints of the people who walked beside me... some who held my heart gently, and others who left wounds I'm still learning to understand. This book is for them—for every person who shaped me, stretched me, or broke me in ways that pushed me toward the woman I am becoming.

What you'll read in these pages is real. It's not polished or perfect; it's me—unfiltered, honest, and finally ready to tell the truth about what I've lived through. Each chapter is dedicated to a family member who impacted my story, whether through love, laughter, conflict, or pain. Some chapters feel warm, like home. Others ache. But all of them matter, because all of them taught me something about who I am and who God is.

Each chapter is paired with a Bible verse, because as I walked through these seasons, Scripture became my oxygen. God wasn't just watching from afar—He was guiding me, whispering to me, steadying me when I thought I would fall apart. He has been the healer of my wounds and the author of every piece of growth that came from them.

At the end of each chapter, you'll find a letter—my heart on paper— written to the person connected to that part of my story. Some letters are soft, some are heavy, and some carry the kind of honesty that took me years to speak. But they are all rooted in grace. Grace for them, and grace for myself. My prayer is that as you read, you feel permission to face your own story… to let God walk with you through the parts that still hurt.

Thank you for choosing to sit with me in these pages. My hope is that this book reminds you that even when life breaks us in places we didn't expect, God never wastes our pain. There is healing. There is purpose. And there is always—always—hope.

"And we know that in all things God works for the good of those who love Him, who have been called according to His purpose."
— Romans 8:28

1

Pops

Proverbs 17:6 – "The glory of children are their fathers."

It's true. From a young age, even before grade school, I admired my father. His strength, his sternness, the way he demanded attention, not just from children but from adults too, left an impression on everyone around him. I had a certain fear of him, but not the bad kind. I actually enjoyed every second of being in his presence.

I didn't talk much. I didn't ask a lot of questions. I simply observed and soaked him in. I remember the days at the beach, the pool, the park, and the blue house. He never just spent time with me; he made time for every child who was around. My siblings, my cousins, everyone. We had a ball together. Whether we were diving (or being pushed) off a pier, getting thrown into the pool as an improvised swim lesson, running laps on a track, or sharing a meal from Cecibon, he made those moments unforgettable. I still remember the fried chicken, rice and peas, bunnan, and pikliz. He fed the whole crew.

Those are the memories I lived for. Quality time meant more to me than anything else. My mom could never fully understand why I loved him so deeply, but I did. I knew his heart because mine beat with the same rhythm.

When I was in elementary school, he would sit in the back of my classroom, quietly observing me. I'd have no idea he was there until another student tapped me and pointed in his direction. The moment I saw his face, my heart lit up. Those visits meant everything to me, especially because there were times when he had been kept away or denied access to see me in my everyday life.

But my pops didn't let a technicality like not being authorized on my school contact card stop him. He showed up anyway. He found a way. My teachers adored him, my friends admired him, but no one loved him more than I did.

The highlight of my entire school year was when he volunteered to chaperone field trips, especially the youth fair. That was my favorite. I remember how exciting it was to choose who got to be in my group. There was one girl, a known bully, who always picked on others. That day, she raised her hand high, begging, "Pick me, pick me, pick me!" I didn't. And when I chose someone else, she cried like a baby, just like she made other kids cry. Served her right. Thanks for that moment, Dad.

I remember sitting in the blue house, tucked away in one of the living room areas, while my dad patiently taught me my letters and numbers. Everything was going well until I kept mixing up the numbers 6 and 9. That's when he gave me a nice *Zoklo* on the forehead. Yes, Dad, you are not off the hook for that one—I still remember that thump of death. But as much as it stung, it worked. I finally figured out the difference between 6 and 9 that very day. All it took was one lesson. I was determined not to face another day thinking he was disappointed in me, even though he wasn't. That was only how I felt in the moment.

I also remember the car rides we shared, filled with long talks that I mostly listened to in silence. I hardly ever responded, but I heard every word. He told me I would go to college, and though I didn't even know what college was at the time, I held onto that promise and made it my mission. Simply because it came from his mouth, I believed it. He spoke about the importance of family, unity, and making a difference in the world. I took it all in, and those words became part of me.

Proverbs 16:16 – "How much better to get wisdom than gold, to get insight rather than silver!"

I watched my dad in his role as commissioner of Moore Park, and it was clear how much joy he found in teaching and mentoring children. His excitement was contagious, and his love for the youth could not be hidden. He didn't just coach the boys' football team from the sidelines. He ran up and down the field with them, making sure they not only heard his voice but also felt his presence.

To this day, he remains the same man, and his love for the youth is still visible in everything he does. For a long time, I wondered how I ended up in the same field of working with young people. Then I realized the truth. I am him, and he is me. The father I grew up knowing and experiencing is still alive within me, only better now than ever before. He isn't perfect, but his heart is golden.

In the summer of 2004, right before the start of 8th grade, I spent every hour of every day with my dad. I didn't care where we were, what we wore, or whether we were doing anything exciting. Just being with him, talking, and sharing time was more than enough for me.

At the time, I had no idea that life was difficult for him. I didn't know he was carrying hardships. All I knew was that with him I felt safe, at peace, and full of joy. 21 years later, I see the whole picture more clearly. We were sleeping in his old school box Chevy with no AC. We sat in the park and talked. We rode from place to place. We ate at Cecibon or Chef Creole, free of charge because the owners treated us like family. But the truth was, we were never in a home. My dad was homeless, and

5

I didn't even know it. That speaks volumes. His love, his time, and his attention sheltered me so deeply that I was oblivious to the struggle. Money was never needed.

Our last day together that summer became the turning point in my life. I never realized it would be the final time I saw him, because he never told me. But looking back now, his actions told the story. He loved me in a way that felt final, almost as if he knew I would not see him again.

Eight years went by without seeing my dad. We spoke every once in a blue moon, but he was no longer in Florida. I didn't see him again until 2012, and even then, it was only for a few days. Yet in those days, it felt as if he had never left. My siblings, cousins, and his grandchildren all gathered together with food and full of laughter, and for a moment it felt like old times. He still had that gift. When he spoke, people listened.

In those years apart, he had gone from Georgia to the Bahamas and eventually settled in Haiti. Much had transpired in his absence. I have always believed that if he had been present, many of the things I went through would never have happened. In those years, I became a mother at 15, only to lose my child's father and step into single motherhood far too soon. I enrolled in college for two years but came back home empty-handed. I tried again later, starting classes once more, but I quit again because life was hard, and figuring it out alone felt even harder.

Sometimes the only way I could cope was by blocking out how deeply I missed my father. I learned to fill the emptiness with other things—projects, distractions, attempts at new beginnings, but none of them lasted. They were just things I would start but never finish.

At 33 years old, I can truly say that I once felt ready to give up on everything, because deep down I believed my dad had given up on me. I thought he had chosen himself over me. But with time and prayer, I have come to see things differently. I've learned that everything happens for a reason. My selfish view of what my father should have done has been replaced with compassion. I believe God had to distance him from the life he once knew to break him, reshape him, and mold him into the man he was created to be. That is perspective.

One of my favorite ties that binds us now is our communication. My pops and I can talk about almost anything. Sometimes I even have to stop him mid-sentence, because there are things I just don't want to know. He keeps it all the way real, sometimes a little too real. We've had tough and uncomfortable conversations about allegations, rumors, past endeavors, mistakes, regrets, and even goals. Through it all, we hold each other accountable for our choices and actions.

There isn't a single thing anyone can tell me about my father that I don't already know. At one point, I even completed a federal background check, just to be sure we had addressed everything openly. Facing the past together has made our future stronger, and it has made our bond even tighter. And if you haven't caught on by now, yes, I'm a daddy's girl.

Dear Pops,

I want to begin by saying something my younger self didn't always have the courage or the understanding to say: I forgive you for leaving. With time—and a lot of life lived—I've learned that your absence wasn't abandonment. It was survival. You were walking away from a life that could have swallowed you whole, and God was pulling you toward something different, something safer. I think about that often. Every time we video chat, every time I hear your voice through the phone, I'm reminded that if you had stayed in Miami, I might not have a father at all. So even in the distance, I thank God for preserving you.

I've learned that speaking highly of you makes some people uncomfortable, as if a person's past is supposed to erase who they are becoming. But I don't carry their judgment. I see you—your heart, your intentions, the vibrations of hope you spill into every conversation. I see the man who still pours life into the youth, even in seasons when you barely have enough for yourself. I see the man who laughs through hunger and instability, who refuses to let struggle dim his spirit. Pops, you don't just survive—you transform.

Thank you for the time you carved out for me when I was little, talking to me like I was older than I was, planting seeds you hoped would grow one day. I didn't understand much back then, but your words stayed with me. They followed me into adulthood. They strengthened me. And thank you for all the things you taught me—how to swim, how to take risks, and trust the process. Even your extreme lessons had purpose.

Thank you for introducing me to sports before I even knew how to spell half of them. Because of you, I found teams that shaped my childhood, coaches who believed in me, and a love for health and wellness that still matters to me today. And thank you for building Star Vision Academy and Helping Hands of the Caribbean, pulling my credentials into your passion and allowing me to work hand in hand with you in serving Haiti's youth. Watching you dream out loud taught me that vision is a form of faith.

You have always been strong, even when life tried to weaken you. But now I understand strength differently—not just the kind the world demands, but the kind God refines. You held me accountable, placed me on a pedestal when I didn't even know I deserved one, and constantly reminded me of my value.

Pops, God has kept you this long because He's not finished with you. You're innovative, curious, disciplined, and aging with a grace that tells me His favor rests on you. You are a leader with more to give, more to build, more to become.

I love you more deeply than these words can hold. It hurts not being able to sit next to you, hug you, or lay my head on your shoulder like I want to. But I choose to trust the bigger picture. You are exactly where God needs you to be right now.

Until we meet again, I'm holding you close in spirit.

With all my love,
Your Daughter

2

Mommy

Proverbs 23:25 – "Let her who bore you rejoice."

Hmm, where do I even start, Mommy? We've been through it, but we've gotten through it all together. My single-digit years with you were everything. I remember the care and time you poured into braiding my hair, making sure I looked nice for school. You took your time—sometimes forever—with your heavy hands, and I'd end up staying up late watching Unsolved Mysteries while you finished. I was always too scared to fall asleep after.

My favorite styles were the "EVE" braids going straight back or the small individual plaits with weave and beads added to the ends. Everyone thought it was my real hair. You kept my hair fly and made sure I represented you well. Oh, how I wish you were still in your "hairstylist" bag. (Yes, Mom, this is me telling you to get back to it!)

Graduations and award ceremonies were unforgettable. You pampered me like I was headed to prom. I remember you giving me my first pedicure, carefully polishing my toes while singing and jamming to what I now consider old school music. Every one of those songs is on my playlist today. Thank you for helping to shape my old soul,

Mommy.

I also remember the times you sang to my sister and me. We'd be glued to you, staring in admiration. Your soft, angelic voice made us feel special, seen, and loved. It wrapped around me like a hug. When you weren't around, I'd pretend to be you. I'd line up the couch pillows in the living room as my audience, pop in either your Toni Braxton or Mary J. Blige CD, pull out the lyric sheet from the case, and sing to my imaginary fans just like you sang to us.

I remember the days when I was sick and had to stay home from school. The way my mom cared for me and nursed me back to health is something I will never forget. She made her buttery, creamy oatmeal, and we would sit together watching *Maury* or *Jerry Springer*. Sometimes I would take over the TV and switch it to *Little Bear* or *Franklin*. It still amazes me that I am now an adult with three kids of my own.

When she was on the phone, I would flip back and forth across her stomach or back without a care in the world. Now, when my children do the same to me, I cannot help but laugh, because I remember being that child once. I can still recall her scent. It was refreshing and comforting. I would fall asleep almost instantly, and then she would plop her leg over me, heavy enough to keep me still, but I loved every moment of it.

The holidays were always special with her. My mom made it a big deal. She always bought a real Christmas tree, and it was always massive. My sister and I helped decorate, but the excitement of gifts was rarely a surprise. My mom could not keep a secret. She would wrap presents right in front of us. Every holiday, she made sure we were dressed in the latest styles. Whether it was BONGO, Limited Too, or Tommy Hilfiger, we were always fly. And with her serving as our personal hairstylist, the look was always complete.

That was also when I discovered my love for platinum jewelry. My mom made sure I had a charm bracelet with a matching necklace and earrings. I will never forget going to a Christmas party and leaving with only one charm still on the bracelet. My jewelry phase ended quickly that night.

I remember the movie nights at Muvico, Sunset, or the drive-in theater. And if we wanted to stay home, there were always Blockbuster movie rentals. Because I value those moments so much, I am still a movie person today, and I have passed that love on to my children. We enjoy watching movies together while eating home-baked brownies, just like the cozy nights I had growing up.

I remember the fine dining restaurants, well, at least they felt like fine dining at that time. I remember the trips to Orlando every year with my Girl Scouts crew. And most importantly, I remember going to church every single Sunday. It was because of my mother that the seeds of Christian faith were planted in me. And it was because of her influence that when I was 15 years old and faced one of the most traumatic experiences of my life, I knew exactly who to call on. Without hesitation, I called on God.

My mother never missed when it came to her home-cooked meals. Fast food was rare in our house because she cooked all the time, not just for us but for everyone who stopped by. Her macaroni and cheese, cheesy, rich, and unforgettable, was always my favorite. I strongly believe that my macaroni and cheese can compete with hers now, but I know I learned from the best.

Then there was the cleaning. If you grew up with a mother who had what I like to call "Obsessive Cleaning Disorder," then you already know where this is headed. She would come into my sister's and my room, pull everything out of the closets, drag out the piles I had hidden under the bed (my favorite dump site back then), empty the dresser drawers, and command us to clean nearly every weekend. At first, we would be upset, but once she turned on her oldie-goldies music, we were hooked. We sang along, cleaning and laughing, and before long, the whole chore turned into a rhythm of joy.

Now, when my son points out that I do the same things she did, all I can do is laugh. The apple really doesn't fall far from the tree. What good memories.

Deuteronomy 4:9 – "Only be careful, and watch yourselves closely so that you do not forget the things your eyes have seen or let them fade from your heart as long as you live. Teach them to your children and to their children after them."

My early childhood years, from birth to eleven, were delightful. I keep those memories stored in my heart, and they continue to inspire me to create a loving environment and impactful moments with my own children. But as I stepped into my preteen and middle school years, everything began to shift. This stage is difficult for any child, but for me, it came with a sudden change. I often wonder if something truly changed in my home or if it was simply that my mind had matured and I was able to see things more clearly. Either way, something happened.

A new individual, my mother's romantic partner, came into our lives for the next four to five years, and the world I once knew was no longer the same. There were good times woven into the difficult ones, but in that season, my feelings of neglect and lack of attention from my mother began to form. Her physical presence was there, but the strength and advocacy I had once admired in her felt absent. She no longer made things happen. It was as if she had stopped trying.

When my sister and I wanted to hang out with friends or do anything outside our home, we had to wait until she asked permission from this person. Most of the time, the answer was no. My mother was dependent on this individual, which meant her decisions for us were no longer her own. That dependence stripped away the admiration I had for her, and the safe space she once provided began to close in around me.

Looking back, I can see that this was the birthplace of my quest for early independence. It was also where I learned to promise myself that when I became a mother, my children would never question my presence. Today, I strive to give them everything they need, some of what they want, and all of me, my full attention, my full presence, my unwavering support. I want them to always know they are loved, seen, and heard. Because I remember what it felt like not to be.

How ironic that in 2004, the same year my father disappeared from my life, neglect was added to my "trauma list." It felt like the abandonment he left behind was now being mirrored in another form.

That year, I moved in with a friend of my mother's so I could attend a new middle school. I hated my old one, and though this was my idea, I still needed my mother to provide for me. I needed hygiene products, clothing, shoes, lunch money, and most of all, food. The family I lived with had two children, and I became close with them. Yet I could not help noticing how their mother provided for them, or at least for one of them, in ways that I desperately longed for.

I was only about twenty to twenty-five minutes away from home, so I never understood why my mother did not send money or ask me what I needed. I never asked her for anything, because deep down I thought I should not have to. Wasn't she supposed to already know? Looking back now, I realize she was wrapped up in her own struggles within her relationship. But that does not erase the reality of how I felt then; for me, it was neglect. I felt forgotten, thrown away, and soon even the family I was staying with began to treat me as if I were less than.

Eventually, I returned home after disagreements about how I was being treated. And while so much of that season carries pain, one thing I can say is that my mother has always had my back when there is conflict. She may have faltered in other ways, but when a fight came, she showed up for me, ready for war.

Going into my freshman year of high school, my mother and her partner split up. I was happy to be back home, and for the first time in years, things started to feel like old times.

And then she met someone else.

This new partner was the complete opposite of the last one. They were fun, gave us allowance, took us out, and most importantly, my mother seemed happy again. For a while, life felt lighter. But eventually she began spending more time at her partner's house than at home. Once again, a part of her was missing in the moments I needed her most. She would drop off groceries to my sister and me every week, but she wouldn't stay. She would leave again.

At the time, I was about fourteen years old, and at first, I didn't see anything wrong with the arrangement. I had freedom. Thankfully, I was self-motivated. I loved school, I joined extracurricular activities like cheerleading, and I made it my business to get up and go to school every day. But I also had a boyfriend. He started coming over daily, and before long, his visits turned into sleepovers, which eventually turned into him practically living with us. I didn't sneak him into the house; I never had to, because my mother wasn't home.

This went on for about a year. Then I became pregnant. Fifteen years old, pregnant.

When I told my mother, she was devastated. She cried and told me I could not keep the baby. I hadn't planned it, but I hadn't prevented it either. I was young and naive, but I would never call myself dumb. My baby's father and I argued with my mother. We wanted to keep the baby, but she wanted us to terminate the pregnancy.

Eventually, she changed her mind, but as the reality set in, both my boyfriend and I began having serious conversations about what raising a child would really take. I started to think about the activities I might miss out on, and together we decided we would go through with an abortion. The problem was that we had no money. In the end, my mother refused. It was too late. I was too far along.

During my pregnancy, my mother and my baby's father argued about everything: the name of the child, how often he came over, even the doctor's appointments. I was drained, so I let them battle it out on their own. What confused me most was how suddenly my mother's attitude toward him changed. She wasn't nice to him anymore, and I could not understand why. By then, it was too late for hostility; the damage had already been done.

Even with all that tension, one thing I can say is that my mother stuck it through with me. She was carrying her own child at the time and managing a high-risk pregnancy herself, yet she still showed up for me at every step. She went to every doctor's appointment, supported me through every ache and pain, stood by me during childbirth, and even cared for my son so that I could continue going to school.

There were good times and bad times, and yes, under different circumstances, my life might have taken a completely different path. But I choose to hold on to the truth that we survived. Because of my mother's support with my son, I never missed a school activity. I was able to keep cheering, attend every senior event, and I never once considered dropping out. If anything, it motivated me even more.

It truly takes a village.

Throughout the remainder of my high school years and the beginning of college, from ages fifteen to eighteen, my mother and I went through a lot. It often felt like a constant war between us. By then, I had learned not to depend on her; the days of leaning on my mother for support were long gone.

I can't even tell you how I managed it all how I paid my phone bill each month. How I got new clothing and shoes for school. How I provided for my son. How I attended every senior event. How I kept my hair done, even though by that time she had given up on being a hairstylist. What I do remember is how alone I felt, as if I were entirely on my own. Yes, she provided a roof over my head, but that was where it ended.

It's all about perspective, though. Because of how I felt in those years, I learned independence. I became resourceful. I discovered the courage to step out in faith and take risks. I came to believe that in every situation, there is a lesson. Things are not simply happening to me; they are happening for me. Learning to stay optimistic and seeing God's hand in everything carried me a long way. I've always chosen to view myself as a victor, not a victim.

And the truth is, in many ways, I am like my mother. I accept that, and I take pride in it. Her life, and everything we have endured together, shaped me into the mother I am today. I've shared some of the negatives, but I chose to turn them into positives. I made the choice to grow rather than linger in the past. I am alive, I am well, I have failed, I have accomplished, I have taken accountability, and I have forgiven what has hurt me or contributed to some of my failures.

Dear Mommy,

There are pieces of my childhood that I still carry with me—some heavy, some tender, all of them shaping the woman I became. If anything I've said has stirred emotions in you, please know this: I never meant to wound you. I was only trying to speak the truth of my own experience, the way a woman looks back on her younger self and finally finds the courage to name what once hurt her. I love you. I respect you. And I forgive you—for what happened, for what didn't happen, for what you simply didn't have the tools to give.

Now that I am older, I see you differently. I see the young woman behind the title "Mama," trying to raise two hormonal teenagers while still learning herself. I see the girl in you who was never truly protected, who was not given the softness or the safety she deserved. And through that lens, my compassion for you has only grown. You were doing the best you could with the pain you inherited and the guidance you never received.

Thank you for stepping in as a second mother to my son when I was still growing up myself. Thank you for caring for him so I could finish high school, for keeping him safe so I could experience the taste of independence in college. Every time I moved, you showed up—even if it was inconvenient, even if life was already heavy on your shoulders. I will never forget that sacrifice. I will never forget that love.

I know you are still carrying the weight of old wounds—ones that were never bandaged, never tended to, never spoken aloud. I don't blame you for the ways those wounds shaped our home. I know now that nothing you did was intentionally harmful. You simply weren't mothered the way you needed to be. You were poured out before you were ever poured into.

Mommy, I want you to know that I still need you. I still crave the comfort of your scent, the familiarity of your presence. To me, you are one of the most talented women walking this earth, even if you don't always see it in yourself. I pray that you grow to believe in your own brilliance. I pray that the compassion I feel for you in my heart begins to reach you in our conversations, in our moments, in the small ways I try my best to love you better.

Life has not been easy for you, but you have already survived every one of your hardest days. It's time to loosen your grip on the past and step into the woman God designed you to be from the very beginning. I don't just want you to smile—I want you to find rest. Real rest. The kind that settles in your spirit and reminds you that you don't have to fight every battle alone.

Matthew 11:28–30 - "Come to me, all you who are weary and burdened, and I will give you rest... and you will find rest for your souls."

I love you more than words could ever stretch to say. And I will always be your daughter—still rooting for you, still praying for you, still loving you with everything in me.

With love,
  Your Daughter

3

Other Half

1 John 2:9 – "Anyone who loves their brother or sister lives in the light, and there is nothing in them to make them stumble."

The salt to my pepper, the yin to my yang, my other half indeed. I love my sister deeply, always have and always will. We are day and night, literally, but somehow we are so much alike at the same time. When we talk, we are so in sync that we finish each other's sentences, make the same sounds, and even say the same things at the same time. Now that I think about it, it is actually kind of weird, but it is also the tie that binds us together.

Even to this day, when people see us together, we still hear the same ignorant and exhausting comment we have endured for over a decade: "Y'all look just alike, she's just light-skinned and you're black." The first part is fine, but the second part is unnecessary and offensive. Like, duh, we do not need that sorry excuse of a comment to remind us of our differences. When I was younger, I disliked my skin tone because people with lighter skin complexions were linked to being more beautiful-so where did that leave me? My family reminded me everyday of how beautiful I was. They'd compliment the richness of my skin tone, how smooth it was, and I'd be referred to as "Black Barbie, or Chocolate Princess." Though I didn't think I was ugly, I was always reminded of our differences. Today, it doesn't bother me at all...now back to my sister.

Growing up, I always wanted to go wherever she went. While she did not agree with this, she knew our mother would only let her go out with friends if she took me along. That is part of the reason I never cared to make friends of my own, her friends were my big sisters, and that was all I needed.

She would often be mean to me in front of her friends, but they always encouraged her to stop and reminded her that it was fine if I hung out with them. Eventually, she stopped making it a fight, and started using my presence to her advantage. I became her alibi when she wanted to sneak off somewhere else instead of where she told our mother she would be. I kept all her secrets, even took spankings for her when my mother found out she was lying, because I refused to tell on her.

I must admit, she was not always the best example for me to follow, but I still wanted to be with her. Even though I was younger, I felt like it was my responsibility to protect her, whether she chose to protect me or not.

My sister hates it when I bring up the stories of how she traumatized me as a child, but she needs to hear them. Why would she do that to "little ole me?" I won't expose everything, but I'll share just a few incidents so you get an idea of my experiences—sorry, sis.

For some reason, she thought it was funny to put a pillow on my head and sit on it. This happened more than once. She would laugh, and although I was confused about what was so funny, I went along with it and laughed too. The truth is, I was a little intimidated by her, and so were her friends. Honestly, I don't even know how she had friends, because she gave them attitude too.

One day, she placed the pillow over my head, sat on it, and when I started kicking and trying to push her off, she didn't budge. Instead, she pressed all her weight down. I felt like I was about to die, at least that's how it seemed to me. Usually, she would get up, but that day she was on "demon time." I felt uneasy, and for the first time, I ratted her out to our mother.

I remember it like it was yesterday. My mother saw how distraught I was, and since I almost never told on my sister, she acted quickly. She called my sister over and said, "Come here, let me show you how it feels." She made her lie down on the couch, placed the pillow over her head, and sat there for a while. The moment I saw my sister's face turn red as she sobbed, a rare sight, since she never even cried during spankings, I felt guilty. Why was I feeling bad when I had done nothing wrong?

Another memory that stands out comes from our elementary school years. I was in third grade and she was in fifth. She was in charge of ironing our school clothes. Most of my uniforms ended up thrown in a corner with holes burned in them, just like my toes. Let me explain. Instead of waking me up by calling my name or nudging me, she would take the iron and press it against the tips of my toes until I jumped up from the burning sensation. She thought it was hilarious. She had no remorse, and in those moments, I was convinced she hated me.

This happened more than once, and no, I never told. I must have had a case of Stockholm syndrome because I still worshiped the ground she walked on. I thought she loved me back, but the evidence often proved otherwise. She took every opportunity to get me in trouble. Sometimes she would even set me up, teaching me to do something wrong, then running to get our mother so she could catch me in the act. I just didn't get it.

As I grew older, the whole "my sister's keeper" phase came to an end. By middle school, I was ready for war, it was time to fight back. The incident that broke the camel's back was when we fought over the cordless phone. Y'all remember those? Back then, we didn't have cell phones of our own, so we took turns using the house phone.

One day, "Miss Thang" forced me off the phone, dragged me by my hair, and pulled me down the hallway. It all happened so fast. By the time I got to my feet, she realized I was finally ready to fight back. She ran into the bathroom and stayed in there just long enough for me to lose interest. But from that moment on, everything changed. I got my lick back every time. No more nice Star.

Don't get me wrong, when it came to outsiders, we always had each other's backs. We just weren't as close behind closed doors. Our mother constantly lectured us about loving each other, not fighting one another, and saving our fights for others if necessary. It took time for us to learn the real meaning of sisterhood.

For some reason, everything shifted during my tenth-grade year. That was the year I was pregnant with my firstborn. When my sister first found out, she was angry with me and even tried to convince our mother not to let me keep the baby. But as my pregnancy progressed, she softened. She started bringing me along on her date nights, inviting me to hang out with her and her friends, and even showing affection.

It felt strange at first, but I didn't dwell on how unfamiliar it was. This was what I had wanted all along, for her to see me as her sweet little sister, the one who loved her deeply and would do anything for her. Since then, everything has changed. We have become each other's diary, closer than white on rice. We talk on the phone almost every day for hours. The terror I once knew has become my refuge.

My sister is sweet, selfless, and would give anyone the shirt off her back. She is still feisty, but now she is also loving, cuddly, and the funniest person I know.

Dear Other Half,

When I look back over my life, the seasons that felt the heaviest were always softened by your presence. Thank you for the long conversations that stretched into the night, the ones where you let me spill my mess without ever making me feel messy. Thank you for listening with a heart that never judged, for the way you lift me with laughter, and for giving me a place where I can be my goofiest, truest self without hesitation.

Some of my sweetest memories live in the kitchen with you—pots simmering, music playing too loud, us cracking jokes and moving around each other like we've been doing this for a lifetime. Those moments felt like home, like God reminding me that family isn't just shared blood, but shared soul.

I want you to know that I see you. All of you. And I love you beyond measure. I pray for the day you fully recognize the power and potential God folded into your being. There are gifts inside you—deep, divine, undeniable—that the world has yet to witness. I pray you rise above fear and step boldly into the life He has written for you. And I pray you continue being the remarkable mother you already are, guiding your children with the wisdom we had to learn the hard way.

May you seek God with a renewed hunger so He can unlock the purpose that has been waiting for you all along. And may we, side by side, break every generational chain that tried to follow us. Because of the sacrifice of our Lord and Savior, we are never denied. Delay is not denial, and it is never too late to reach for greatness.

And just so you never forget: I still worship the ground you walk on, and I love you infinitely.

With love,
    Your Other Half

4

Brother

1 John 4:20-21 – "If anyone says, 'I love God,' but hates his brother, he is a liar. For whoever does not love his brother, whom he has seen, cannot love God, whom he has not seen. And he has given us this command: Anyone who loves God must also love his brother and sister."

When I learned that my mother was pregnant at the same time I was carrying my firstborn, something inside me immediately told me her child would be a boy. Inwardly, I hoped it would not be. Part of me even wished she would choose not to have him, because I felt she was too old to be starting over (which was ridiculous, since she was only in her thirties). In my teenage mind, she should have been focused on being a grandmother to my unborn child, though I had no business being pregnant myself at just fifteen years old.

Deep down, I knew my mother had always longed for a son. With me pregnant with a boy as well, I could already foresee the tension and competition it might create between us. At around five months, we learned the truth: she was indeed having a boy. I was happy for her, and I knew our children would share a special bond, but in the back of my mind, I was troubled about what this meant for the future of our relationship.

While my mother carried the child she had prayed for and yearned for, my brother had to endure some difficult challenges even in the womb. It upset me deeply. I did not understand the purpose of praying and longing for a child, only to bring him into circumstances that did not feel safe or fair. Yet by God's grace, and with the help of a medically necessary cerclage that kept him in the womb full-term, he survived. He made it.

I remember being at cheer practice and receiving videos of this beautiful baby boy. I immediately wanted to kiss his chunky cheeks, run my fingers through his thick, curly hair, and breathe in his newness. My baby brother, the cutest newborn I had ever seen. From the start, he carried the same laid-back vibe he still has today, with just a touch of craziness if you happened to upset him.

I remember him lying quietly on a pillow, simply observing. Everyone was afraid to feed him because of his severe reflux. Any bottle he drank was almost guaranteed to come back up in your face or all over your clothes. For the first six or seven months, he rarely made sounds or showed much expression. I must admit, I worried something was wrong. Maybe he was delayed. I would try to engage him and play with him, but there was no emotional response, only puke if I shook him up too much. Forming an emotional connection in those early stages was difficult, but I never stopped trying.

My brother and my firstborn were only three months apart. They woke up at the same time, pooped at the same time, and did almost everything in unison, like twins. My brother would watch my son's independence as he moved around the house, then reach out to grab his leg as if to say, "Take me with you, I want to walk too." Soon after, my brother began to interact more. He started walking and expressing himself. Thank God, because we had all been worried. But with a name like his, Nehemiah, we should have known that God had already spoken purpose over him.

As my brother and my son grew, they were raised like brothers. They dressed alike, went everywhere together, and even though they sometimes had different interests or were treated differently, they loved each other and were inseparable.

But not all the memories are easy. I don't know if the children can remember, but many of the fights between my mother and me centered around them. I often felt that nothing I did for my brother was ever enough in her eyes. Just trying to provide for my own son was a struggle. I would sneak clothing into the house that I had bought for him, afraid my mother would get upset if I hadn't purchased the same for my brother. I had no job, was still a student, and survived on only $150 a month in cash assistance, of which $50 went to my mother. How could I possibly provide for two children and myself?

I understood that she had to provide for my son as well as her own child, but the weight of it made me feel guilty for not being able to do more. At the same time, I wished she would have seen things from my perspective. I was doing my best as a teenage mother, but I was still a child myself.

The children shared toys, but whenever a disagreement broke out that ended with my brother crying or throwing a tantrum, my son was always seen as the one in the wrong. This set the tone early on; my brother learned that he could have his way because our mother would always side with him. That constant dilemma made it unbearable to live with her, and it created tension that made it difficult for my brother and me to build a strong relationship.

During arguments, my mother would say things that suggested I did not love or care for him, often while he was standing right there. Imagine hearing that repeatedly over the years; how could he not begin to believe it? I remember when she turned the bedroom my sister and I shared into a boy's room while we were still living there. She painted it blue and red for our brother, completely dismissing how we might feel. Our hearts were crushed. It was as if she were telling us to get out, and truthfully, she had said those exact words on more than one occasion. The boldness of her actions revealed what she really felt. My sister and I responded by moving in with friends or boyfriends, doing whatever we could to escape a place that no longer felt like home.

I never blamed my brother for any of this, but because I was away so often, I fear he may have felt like I did not care. It was never about him. It was about the actions of our mother toward me, especially when those actions involved him.

Today, my brother and I are not as close as I would like. I love him deeply, though I am not sure he realizes just how much. There are times I call or text, and he does not respond, and it hurts. I have never had ill will toward him. I want him to live a good life and be surrounded by things that are positive and uplifting. In the past, I even asked if he could live with me so I could help nurture his gifts and interests, but my mother refused.

Now both my brother and my son are teenagers, the same age. They could be reaching for the stars together, chasing dreams side by side. Instead, life has turned out differently. The love between them remains, and they still communicate, but they rarely spend time together, and their paths have drifted apart.

When I see my brother, I often find myself more upset with myself than with him. I get frustrated that I am not yet where I want to be in life, stable enough to raise him the way I have raised my own children. In my life, every day feels like a new adventure. There are always mountains to climb, trials to endure, and storms to push through. And all of that reduces my flexibility to help and do as much for my family as I would like.

I remember one moment in 2023, a very trying year for me, the year that, in many ways, felt like the start of my fall from grace (I say that dramatically, but it truly was not my best year). My brother texted me and asked if I could send him five dollars. Just five dollars. And I cried because, at that moment, I truly didn't have it. I felt like a failure. To him, it may have looked like I was making excuses, but the truth is I was at one of the lowest points of my life.

I was paying $2,700 in rent, with over $5,000 in monthly expenses, and my only income was coming from DoorDash and the occasional shift as a bottle girl at an event space. I was living off credit cards, drowning in debt, going through a divorce, and struggling to put food on the table for my own children. Usually, when my brother asked for money, I would send him more than he requested. But that day I couldn't. And from then on, he never asked me for anything again, not since the first time I ever said no.

I cannot blame him. But the truth is, it still breaks my heart. How pathetic did I feel, not even being able to come up with five dollars? Sad.

Dear Brother,

When I think of you as a little boy—six, maybe seven—I can still see that spark in your eyes, the kind of light that made the whole house feel full. You'd sit at those drums and play like you were performing for the world, loud enough to rattle the walls and get on everybody's nerves, but even then, I knew it meant something. There was purpose in that noise. And that same gentle heart that loved animals back then—the stray cats, the random dogs you continue to sneak in the house—is just who you are. A heart like yours says a lot without speaking: kindness, softness, and a quiet willingness to give of yourself.

I pray that God aligns your steps with His purpose, that you get to experience what it feels like to walk in a calling that fits you like your own skin. I pray you break free from anything designed to make you feel small, trapped, or unworthy of the dreams planted in your spirit. Forget what everyone else is chasing. Use what's already in your hands. Plant your own seeds and trust that they will grow into something good.

I also want to say this: I'm sorry for the times I haven't been the sister you needed. Sometimes the things I want for our family feel too big, too far away, like dreams I can see but can't reach just yet. But please don't ever mistake distance for absence. I'm here—one phone call, one thirty-minute drive away. I want more with you: more conversations, more honesty, more closeness. I want you to tell me what you need, what you're struggling with, what's been sitting heavy on your mind.

When I was your age, I remember feeling lost, too—uncertain, stretched thin between who I was and who I hoped God was shaping me to be. What pulled me through was taking chances, asking questions, walking straight into mistakes, learning how to get back up, and surrendering all that fear to God. If I could hand you one thing from my journey, it would be that: the courage to keep going even when you feel unsure.

Watching you with your nieces and nephews warms me in a way I can't fully explain. You let them tackle you, climb on your neck, and double-team you without complaint—just laughing, patient, present. You've always had that big-brother energy: cool, steady, loving in your own quiet way.

I know God has something bigger waiting for you. And when that moment comes, you'll rise into it like you were meant for it all along. Never forget this: you are loved, you are needed, you are capable, and you are more than enough. Your sisters speak so highly of you—always. And it breaks our hearts that we aren't as close as we want to be. But the door is open. Our arms are open. We are here for you, no matter what.

We love you, our Big Little Brother.

James 5:9 — "Don't grumble against one another, brothers and sisters,

or you will be judged. The Judge is standing at the door!"

Romans 12:10 — "Love one another with brotherly affection. Outdo one another in showing honor."

With love,
  Your Sister

5

First Love

Psalm 34:18 – "The Lord is near to the brokenhearted and saves those who are crushed in spirit."

My first love and I met in seventh grade at Charles R. Drew Middle School. We shared the same homeroom class. I can't remember the teacher's name, but I do remember it was in the wood shop room. I can see it like it was yesterday. During a statewide assessment, at the time known as FCAT, we had some free time, and a group of us decided to play spin the bottle in the back room.

I thought he was the cutest thing I had ever seen. He had pearly white teeth, a beautiful smile, dimples, smooth caramel skin, and an Afro neatly picked out. We just kept smiling at each other across the table. Then someone spun the bottle, and of course, it landed on us. The group dared us to go into the closet to kiss. We went in, but instead of kissing, we just talked. That's when he asked me to be his girlfriend.

I walked into that closet, crushing, and I came out taken, look at God. From then on, he would walk me home almost every day. The last time he walked me home, though, he tried to persuade me to let him inside. It made me uncomfortable. We had talked about sexual things before, but I wasn't ready. So I dumped him that day. He was too much for me. Not long after, he transferred to another school. Looking back, it all worked out for the best.

Fast forward two years. We were now in high school, and I had just transferred from Miramar High to Booker T. Washington. I walked into my new reading class, and the very first person I saw in the back, smiling from ear to ear, was my first love.

Now I know what you're thinking, "aww, it was meant to be." But that was not what went through my head. My first thought was to run far away from him, because his reputation with me was still clouded by how fast he had been when we were younger.

For the first two months, he tried every day to get my number. He even sent his friends to convince me to give him a chance, but my answer was always no.

Then one day, after cheerleading practice, I came home, ran my bath water, and soaked for over an hour—that was my daily routine. When I finally got out, dried off, wrapped a towel around me, and opened the door, there he was. Sitting on my couch, smiling from ear to ear—my first love, again.

I froze. My mind raced through the questions, who, what, when, how, and why. I dashed into my mother's room, threw on some clothes, and called for my sister to explain. At the time, she was dating his cousin, and once he found out we were related, he made his move. My sister gave in, told him where we lived, and he caught the bus over. And y'all, he had to be patient—because I had been soaking in that tub for more than an hour. That alone earned him some points.

When I finally built up the courage to come out, I sat beside him, and we talked for hours. That was when I realized how smart he was. We discussed all kinds of topics, and little by little, the judgment I had carried about his past faded away. He was someone of substance—someone I could relate to and actually enjoy.

Before he left, he asked me to be his girlfriend. I told him that Valentine's Day was the following day, and if he came with a gift, I'd say yes. Sure enough, he showed up to school with the biggest teddy bear, roses, and that infamous heart-shaped box of chocolates. From that day on, I was in love with him, and there was nothing anyone could say to change my mind.

At school, my first love and I were never the show-off type. We didn't hold hands in the hallway or put on displays of affection. Most days, it was just a smile or a quick hello. We saved the mushy stuff for when we were alone.

During that season, my mother was rarely home, so he came over nearly every day. We were intimate—because with that much freedom, it almost felt inevitable.

Not long after, he dropped out of school. As smart as he was, I couldn't understand it at the time. Looking back, I see it differently. He was one of ten siblings, his mother was barely staying afloat, and as one of the eldest sons, he felt pressure to help provide. At just sixteen, he turned to the streets. I wasn't happy about it, but I felt powerless to stop him.

Eventually, I became pregnant. For most of my pregnancy, he was in and out of juvenile detention, stealing cars, and caught with drugs. Sometimes it was just a few days, sometimes weeks. But whenever he got out, he tried to show up for me. He would bring me food, McDonald's passed through the school gate, breakfast or lunch dropped off when he could. One day during our food exchange, I begged him to come back to school. He looked at me, paused for a minute, then made a statement about needing money for our baby..

Meanwhile, he and my mother argued constantly about the baby's name. He wanted a junior; she insisted on something different. That tension only deepened my frustration with him, especially since he didn't attend appointments or even the baby shower. He would say that the dads aren't supposed to go to things like that; some of the guys from the neighborhood had fed him those lies, and him, not knowing any better, believed it was true. He really didn't make the situation any better between him and my mother, saying foolish things like that.

The night of my baby shower, I went into labor. My mother yelled at him over the phone to make sure he showed up at the hospital, and he did. But once there, he didn't know how to comfort me. I was in pain, with no epidural, and I acted out badly. He sat quietly, torn between laughing and crying, just staring at me as I pushed through the highs and lows of childbirth. His gaze was full of admiration. He couldn't believe what it took. The next day, he told me how much more his love had grown after seeing our son come into the world.

We went down to medical records to fill out the birth certificate, and that's when I discovered he didn't know his own social security number. He said he had to call his mother. I was embarrassed. We had just brought a child into the world, and yet in that moment, I realized I couldn't afford for either of us to stay children any longer.

That day, a switch flipped. I was in mommy mode, and I needed him to rise into daddy mode. I had the hard conversation with him about making better choices. I told him he needed to get out of the streets, find a job, and focus on providing for our son. I warned him that if he kept getting locked up, I wouldn't be the little girl crying on the phone anymore. I was done. It was time to grow up.

For the first time, he didn't argue. He knew I was right. Within days, he and his father dropped off employment applications at my house. Slowly but surely, he started changing. I could see he wanted to be a good father, and he didn't want to lose me. Usually, his stubbornness made him brush off my suggestions, but now he listened. He became more affectionate. Step by step, he was growing.

In October 2007, it was homecoming month at our high school, and we had a dance. I went, and for the very first time, he stayed home alone with the baby. Poor daddy, our son gave him a hard time. He called me all night, saying the baby wouldn't stop crying and that he had been walking up and down the block trying to calm him. I told him everything would be fine, just stick it out, and that I'd be home soon.

The next morning, as we were getting ready for church, my phone rang at 7 a.m. Who even calls that early? It turned out to be a guy I had given my number to at homecoming. My first love answered the phone. When I walked into the room, he was furious. He told me what happened, and I remember his words verbatim: "Tell him he can have you, because I don't want you anymore!"

I laughed—not because it was funny, but because finally he got a taste of what I had felt when he cheated on me with one of my close friends. He always denied it, but that ex-friend told me everything. And here I was, not even cheating, just guilty of giving out my number. Honestly, I didn't even know why I did it, because I was crazy about him.

For two days, we stayed broken up, though we still talked. He dumped me on Sunday, October 28, 2007. By Tuesday, October 30, he was asking for me back. It was an early release day, and I already had plans to go to the movies with my cheerleading team. He called and asked me to meet him at his dad's house. I told him no, just come to my mother's house instead, so he could see the baby too.

Before hanging up, he asked, "Are you gonna be my girl again?"

Dragging it out, I said, "I'll tell you when I see you at the house later."

That's when he made a comment that still haunts me. He said, "Tell me now, it might be too late."

At the time, it didn't make sense. I brushed it off, repeated that I'd tell him later. In my heart, the answer was already yes. But I was playing hard to get. For so long, he had wrapped me around his finger, and now I wanted to feel like I had control. We were young, silly, and didn't know any better.

Oh, how I wish I had put my pride aside—met him at his father's house, or simply told him yes when he asked me to be his girlfriend again. Because that turned out to be the last day I ever heard his voice.

I remember waiting on the porch for him to come over. He had just called and said he was on his way. Our son was in his swing, and I sat listening to Beyoncé's "Broken-Hearted Girl" on repeat. Less than thirty minutes later, one of my friends called with the worst news of my life. She was screaming through the phone that my first love had been shot at a store. She said he was lying there, fighting for his life.

I ran into the house, screaming, which startled the baby, and he began crying too. My mom jumped out of the shower, soap still on her, rushing to see what was wrong. When I told her, she wrapped her arms around me as I collapsed into shock.

A few moments later, my phone rang again. The same friend told me the police had finally arrived. She said they took a while, and as they lifted him onto the gurney, she saw him take his last breath.

I couldn't process it. I had just spoken to him. How could he be gone? Dead. Never coming back. In that moment, his words echoed in my head: "Tell me now, it might be too late."

Did he know? Did he sense something? Or was it just a coincidence that the wrong words came out at the right time? Either way, I didn't listen. And the guilt consumed me. I went down a rabbit hole of blame. If only I had met him at his father's house, he wouldn't have been at that store. He would still be here with us.

When I arrived at the scene, the skies opened up and rain poured down. His blood washed away into the street, but his bike was still there, lying tipped over on the ground. He rode that bike everywhere, and the sight of it abandoned told me all I needed to know. I cried and screamed in the rain, refusing to leave the last place his presence had touched.

I can't remember if his brother showed up at the scene or if he called me, but I still hear his voice crying in my ear: "He's gone, Star. He left us, Star!" I broke down all over again.

I had to pull myself together long enough to get the baby out of the rain. Soon we were asked to go down to the police station. My mom stayed out front with the baby while I was taken to the back room with a detective. The questions felt endless. He assumed my first love had been in a gang, that he had enemies, that he was caught up in the streets. I had no knowledge of any of it, but they kept pressing, growing verbally aggressive as though trying to break me down.

I sat in that interrogation room forever. I cried, then dozed off in exhaustion, then woke to cry again. At one point, I asked the detective through tears if it was all real, if he was truly gone. The answer was yes. The sad reality was that my son would never get the chance to grow up with his father. That truth hit me like a stone: grief.

Matthew 5:4 - says, "Blessed are those who mourn, for they will be comforted."

Yes, God comforted me. He gave me peace and strength, two things I didn't know I would desperately need. That season was my first personal encounter with God. I prayed, I cried, I talked to Him because I had no clue what else to do.

I wanted my first love back, but I knew that wasn't possible. So I begged God to take the pain away. The relief wasn't immediate, but slowly, over time, it came. What God gave me right away was the strength to carry on for our son, and a peace that allowed me to accept my life would never be the same. Because after something so traumatic, how could it be?

As time passed, he would visit me in my dreams on the days that mattered most. Always with that radiant smile stretched from ear to ear. I would see him when our son grew his first tooth, when he took his first steps, and on Valentine's Day, our anniversary. I longed for those dreams. I prayed for them, just to see his face again. I only wish we had been given more time.

Dear First Love,

Seventeen years. Sometimes that number feels impossibly large, like a lifetime stacked on top of another lifetime. Other days it feels small, like the years folded into themselves and brought me right back to the last moment I saw your face. Time plays tricks like that. But whenever doubt creeps in—whenever I wonder if what we had was as real as it felt—I just look at our son. He is your proof. Your echo. Your twin in ways that make my chest tighten and soften at the same time.

People say memories fade, but mine haven't. Not of you. I still hear your voice so deep that it sounds like the quiet storm, late-night radio host. I still see that smile, and remember how it made me smile even when I was mad at you. And Lord, I will never forget that stubborn little crusty bottom lip—why were you so committed to fighting Chapstick? Your son, thankfully, didn't inherit that battle. He is practically a spokesperson for moisturized lips.

So much of him belongs to you. His smile—your dimples. His voice—deep, rich, the kind that settles in a room. Even his personality mirrors you: slow to open up, but warm once he does. Easygoing. Kind. You live in him, and I thank God for that. Thank you for giving me a piece of you to keep.

Can you believe he's about to graduate from high school? You and I never got far enough to dream about cap and gown moments. Now, he asks about you—little things at first, then questions that reveal the weight he carries. He thinks deeply, holds everything inside, like he's trying to protect the world from what he feels. I do my best to fill in the gaps you left behind, but sometimes I wonder if I'm doing enough. Still, when I look at the young man he's becoming, I remind myself: I didn't fail him. Not completely.

I always wished we could have raised him together, in a home full of stability and love. After you, I tried to recreate that picture, but the truth is—I never got it right. He wasn't always reserved. As a child, he was wild and silly, always dancing, always joking. Then something shifted. Maybe it was puberty. Maybe it was my mistakes. Maybe it was the men who walked into our lives but couldn't connect with him. Whatever it was, he started building walls. He learned to be serious, maybe to protect himself. Maybe to protect me. I miss the light he used to let shine, but even now, I admire the strength he carries. And just like you were starting to learn about me—I don't play when it comes to our son.

I pray you're resting in peace. I pray God's mercy covered you then and continues to cover you now. And I pray that when my time here is done, I'll see you again on the other side. I'm grateful I convinced you to take those pictures at Cute Shots; without them, our son wouldn't have anything tangible to hold onto—just stories and the pieces of you he carries in his face.

I could write you pages and still not release everything sitting in my heart, so I'll end here. I love you. We love you. And I miss you in a way that time has not healed.

Gone, but never forgotten.

With love,
   Your Star

6

First Born

Psalm 127:3-4 - "**Children are a heritage from the Lord, offspring a reward from him. Like arrows in the hands of a warrior are children born in one's youth.**"

My firstborn, my love child. He has walked through everything with me. The day I learned I was pregnant, something inside of me shifted. I couldn't hide behind timidness anymore—I had too many questions, too much to learn, and a reason to push forward. I wanted to be the best mother I could be. Everyone around me seemed certain I was throwing my life away. My own family said that having this baby would ruin me, but I was determined to prove that my circumstances would not define me.

Yes, maybe I could have achieved more, or thought further ahead, but my son was meant to be. He is the reason I have come as far as I have. Because of him, I take risks. Because of him, I fight. He is my motivation.

Being fifteen and pregnant came with highs and lows. The hardest parts were the stares, the whispered comments, and the weight of shame that seemed to follow me everywhere. I caught the bus to school with a belly I could no longer hide. I had to give up cheerleading, something that had once been my world. My body changed almost overnight. Fifty pounds piled on, and the first time I saw stretch marks snake across my stomach, I almost fainted. I had been faithful with Palmer's cocoa butter—the kind with the smiling pregnant woman on the bottle—convinced it would save me. But no. What a rip off!

My mother wanted to transfer me to COPE, a school for pregnant girls, but I refused. The idea of being surrounded by other hormonal teenagers didn't sit right with me. I wanted to stay where I was. So I remained at my original high school, determined to finish what I had started. They offered me an elevator key so I wouldn't have to climb the stairs, but I declined. I wanted at least some kind of workout. The lunch ladies looked out for me, too. They gave me extra food, and sometimes my classmates would buy me snacks. No wonder the weight piled on.

During my pregnancy, the library became my sanctuary. It was my safe place, my solace. Honestly, I think I was the only student who even used it—every time I went, it was empty. Reading kept my mind sharp and my imagination alive. It calmed me, gave me satisfaction, and kept me from ever feeling bored. Even now, you'll never hear me say I'm bored, because there's always something to read. I had always been a reader, but pregnancy took it to another level. I had researched that reading to your baby stimulates brain development and lays the foundation for early literacy. I believed it, too, because my son has always been a sharp student. Math has always been his thing, but overall, he has done well in school.

The night of my baby shower, June 23, 2007, I wore a little black sundress with white polka dots and matching sandals. The shower was full of my mother's and sister's friends, because at fifteen, what money did my own friends have for gifts? In truth, it didn't feel like my baby shower. It felt like my mother's party—the adults were drinking and having a good time while I sat there swollen and exhausted. I don't even remember us playing shower games, but I did receive many gifts. My son was blessed before he ever took his first breath.

After the shower, I was determined to go into labor that night. I strolled up and down the block, my swollen feet pounding against the pavement, my darkened neck making me look like I was wearing a permanent black turtleneck. As if that wasn't enough, one of the guests at the shower had shouted across the room, "Ohhh, Star, your neck is black!" Like really? No sympathy for the hormonal, sensitive mommy-to-be?

Eventually, I gave up on walking, took a shower, and laid down. Around four in the morning, I woke to sharp pains in my lower abdomen. Contractions. When I stood to go to the bathroom, my water broke right there on the bedroom floor. I screamed for my mother. She rushed in and told me to get in the shower. I was furious—the contractions were coming fast, and here she was insisting I shower while in pain. To make matters worse, both she and my aunt were tipsy, the blind leading the blind. I had no choice but to follow their lead, praying for strength.

We grabbed my hospital bag and headed for the emergency room. Once we got there, my mother asked the staff for a wheelchair. They were moving too slowly for her liking, because I remember my aunt marching behind the front desk and wheeling away the receptionist's rolling chair. I was in so much pain that I didn't care—I just sat and let them push me along.

When we finally reached the labor and delivery floor, the contractions came one after another with no breaks in between. One minute I was on my knees in the bed, the next I was standing, tossing, turning, moaning, crying—nothing I did made the pain ease. I had gone too far to receive an epidural. My aunt leaned over the bed, trying to coach me through it, but her breath reeked of alcohol. She told me to inhale and exhale, demonstrating it in my face. In anguish, I yelled at her to leave me alone.

The pain and the stench together were unbearable.

Then suddenly, I had the urge to push. The nurse told me to stop, even pushed my legs together, but I barked at her that I couldn't control it. Every push gave me a brief break from the pain, so I pushed anyway. Out came a cone-headed little boy. My mother explained that his head was that way because the nurse kept closing my thighs while he was in the birth canal. She rubbed his head gently until it shaped itself into a perfect round ball, which it has remained to this day.

Three hours of labor felt like an eternity, but at around 7 AM, my baby boy was here. He was so tiny, just over five pounds. Once he was out, the placenta followed, and then my body began to tremble violently. My lips quivered, my teeth chattered, and I couldn't stop shaking. I was terrified something was wrong, but the nurses assured me it was normal—postpartum chills.

A few hours later, when the haze lifted, I became aware of the pain in my bottom. Before discharging me, the nurse insisted I have a bowel movement, but the pain was unbearable. I later learned why: during delivery, the doctor had to cut me from my "roota to my toota," as my mother would say. I wasn't fully developed, and my body didn't open wide enough for the baby to pass. There was no way I was straining against that kind of pain. I lied to the nurse, swore I had gone to the bathroom, just to be released.

By June 26, 2007, I was home, holding my healthy baby boy—Tyrique Omari Williams—in my arms. My firstborn. My everything.

By the time my son was four months old, his father had passed away. The weight of that loss nearly crushed me, but I am truly grateful for my mother and for his father's side of the family. They stepped in and were always present in his life. If I had school or needed a weekend break, they were there. Their support mattered more than they probably knew.

Even with help, every day as a single mother was hard. This wasn't the life I envisioned for myself or my child. But I couldn't dwell on what I couldn't change. While my heart ached for both of us, I had to keep moving forward—for both of us. And slowly, the days did got easier.

I was proud of my beautiful baby boy. I carried his pictures everywhere, showing them off to my classmates. Sometimes I brought him to cheer practice or to school track meets. He was chunky, with the cutest dimples, bowed legs, and feet so pigeon-toed I worried he'd struggle to walk. But he surprised me—he was on his feet by ten months old. He fell often, but he always got back up, determined and unbothered.

Even as a baby, he was self-sufficient in ways that amazed me. During my nightly bathroom trips, I'd place a bottle on my nightstand. By morning, he wouldn't wake me—he'd slide out of bed, grab his bottle, and play quietly until I got up.

Leaving him on school mornings was the hardest. He and I were often the only ones awake in the house. My mother would still be asleep, and sometimes she wouldn't wake for him right away. I'd set out snacks, a juice cup, and turn on the TV so he had something within reach until she stirred. He cried when I left, and I cried inside, too.

Eventually, daycare made things easier. Knowing he was surrounded by other children in a structured environment lifted so much weight from my mind. Still, it was a grind. Every morning before school, I walked him nine blocks to daycare and nine blocks back after. It was a long trek for his little legs, but we never complained. We just did it.

That became the rhythm of our lives—resilience and persistence. My son and I grew up together. Every obstacle I faced, he faced right beside me. Every triumph I had, he shared. Even now, that hasn't changed.

Proverbs 22:6 — "Start children off on the way they should go,

and even when they are old they will not turn from it."

I have always longed to give my son stability. No matter how hard I tried, life had its way of shifting us. We moved in with others, we relocated to different states—twice—and he transferred schools more times than I can count. Yet through it all, he adjusted. Nothing ever dimmed his light or slowed his ability to excel.

Now at thirty-three, I'm still in the fight for stability. But I've learned from my mistakes, and I share those lessons with my son. Whenever I feel the urge to give up, love for him and his siblings keeps me pressing forward. They are my motivation, my reason to work harder, my reason to raise the standard so their futures surpass anything I've ever known.

Our years in Tennessee, when he was between ten and thirteen, marked a season of major adjustment. He attended a Seventh-day Adventist private school, where the students were vegan. Imagine my meat-loving son navigating life without chicken or beef—it was an adventure in itself. At that school, he was one of only two Black children, but he thrived. He sang hymns, prayed, read Scripture, and little by little, spiritual seeds began to take root.

At home, we built our own rhythm of faith. Morning and evening, we gathered for devotionals. We read the Bible, sang songs of praise, and talked about the Word. His curiosity was endless, and the questions he asked about God gave me joy. For once, I felt like I was doing something right. Tennessee gave me the chance to pour into my children without so much of the world's noise, and it gave us a glimpse of peace I will always treasure.

My mother-in-law at the time introduced us to nature and stillness. She had a farm with chickens and a garden, a little oasis that slowed life down. We'd sit together watching Planet Earth and then step outside to see the animals with our own eyes. I believe it was there, in those quiet acres, that his love for animals first began to bloom.

Throughout my son's life, he has had two father figures, but neither connection ever grew into what he needed.

The first provided well. He made sure my son had every new Jordan release, the latest games, clothes, toys—anything a child could ask for. He spent time teaching him football, showed up to every game, and supported him in the best way he knew how. But he was emotionally unavailable. His style was all discipline with no balance of affection, and it broke my heart. I tried to step back, let him father in his own way, and gently offered suggestions that could have strengthened their relationship, but he pushed back every time. Inside, I battled with myself. I was protective of my child, but I also knew I couldn't teach him alone how to be a man. I kept trying to be okay with what I saw and felt—until one day, I simply couldn't anymore.

The second father figure was my ex-husband, who was also my son's godfather. The truth is, he wasn't a kid person. Blinded by love and our history, I didn't see it clearly at first. He was more invested in me than in the children. He didn't follow through on promises, and he rarely considered what they wanted—only what he wanted for them. His discipline was harsh, his affection nearly absent. Having grown up with his own father, I thought he'd reflect on that and do better, but instead, he seemed blind to the compassion my son needed. Too often, he focused on the negative. Over time, I even began to feel that he didn't like my son.

To his credit, he did teach accountability. Through those long, never-ending three-month punishments, my son learned how to study diligently, and I am grateful for that lesson—even though it broke me to watch him endure it. But when the relationship ended, my son confided that he felt my ex-husband hated him. Looking back, I can't dismiss his words. I've come to believe that lack of perspective breeds lack of compassion. I make it my habit to step into other people's shoes, even if I don't agree with them. It helps me understand their "why," and it frees me to live without grudges. Perspective brings peace.

Today, when I look at my son, I am overwhelmed with gratitude that he is mine. Yes, he's expensive, and yes, he annoys me like any teenager, but he is everything I could hope for. He's a leader who thinks for himself. He has self-control, resists peer pressure, and is disciplined in the things that matter to him. He is honest and direct, loyal and hardworking. I've seen him cheer for others with a genuine heart, even while wrestling with his own inner battles.

Since he was four, he has loved football. And like our life's story, his football journey has been filled with hurdles. Yet he leans on his faith in God for strength. My heart swells when I see him spending time with God on his own. That sight lifts a weight from my shoulders because I know when he steps into adulthood, when he leaves for college, he will already be in the safest hands of all.

Dear First Born,

*There are no words wide enough to hold the love I have for you, but still I try. From the moment I met you, you brought light into my life—not the kind that blinds, but the kind that guides. You have been joy to me in a world that has not always been gentle. Even in the seasons that stretched us thin, you stood strong beside me, resilient in ways I didn't always know a child could be. Your quiet faith in God has carried me on days when my own faith felt tired, reminding me that all things truly do work together for good to those who love Him. (**Romans 8:28**)*

*When I look at you, I want to protect you from every heartbreak, every disappointment, every storm that life might one day send your way. But I also know life will shape you the way it shaped me—through both the breaking and the rising. And I've watched you rise, baby. Even when life knocked the wind out of you, you found a way to breathe again. That kind of strength is already inside you. Never forget it. You are loved. You are chosen. You are needed. And you carry greatness because greater is He who is in you. (**1 John***

4:4)

I want to say this clearly, from a mother's heart: I'm sorry for the relationships that didn't work, for the instability they created, for the moments that may have left you confused or uncomfortable. I'm sorry you didn't always have the steady father figure you deserved. None of that was your fault—not one moment of it. And I'm sorry for every move, every reset, every time I had to start over and brought you along for the ride. I hope you know it was never out of carelessness. It was out of survival, of trying to piece together a life that would one day feel whole for both of us.

Every day, I grind to make sure your adulthood will be richer—emotionally, spiritually, and financially—than the childhood you had to navigate. I want your future to be paved with abundance, not struggle. And I pray constantly that you step fully into everything God has designed for you.

I know I've told you this in passing, in hugs, in car rides, and on the days you needed it most—but hear it again: I love you. Deeply. Fiercely. Without pause. I will support you in every dream you chase (unless you're out here doing something illegal, because no—Mommy is not going to jail for you! And if you try to hide a body, I will be the one calling the police). You know my love is real and honest like that.

My prayer is that you live a life overflowing with purpose, joy, and divine alignment. That you rise into the full power of who God created you to be. And that you always know—no matter where life takes you—your mother is cheering for you every step of the way.

Love always,
  Mommy

7

"P"

Proverbs 11:25 - "A generous person will prosper; whoever refreshes others will be refreshed."

Who is "P"? He is my right-hand man, my friend, my business partner, and the best co-parent I could ask for. I have known him for more than fifteen years, and for five of those years, we shared a romantic relationship.

Let's back up. "P" and I first connected in 2010 through Facebook. How we ran across each other online, I honestly do not know. Before then, I had never seen him around, and we did not share friends or family connections. But his posts made me laugh, and if you know me, you know I love to laugh. I am a true goofball. At first, I commented on his posts casually, just responding to the jokes he made. Then he began commenting on mine, until eventually he slid into my DMs. At first, it was just small talk, but soon he asked for my number.

During that time, I was in and out of Tallahassee for college. On one of my visits home, he came along to my cousin's birthday dinner with me and my sister. The whole way to the restaurant, he kept us laughing with joke after joke. That night, he felt cool, comfortable, and easy to be around. Romance was not on my mind yet, but he was definitely a friend I wanted to keep close. As time went on, he showed his generosity again and again. Anything I needed that I could not go to my mom for, he was there. That combination, his humor, his heart, and his giving spirit, slowly pulled me toward him in a deeper way.

A few months later, we started dating. I will never forget our first meet-up as a couple. I had dropped him off at work one morning, and he asked me to go to the mall to grab him a few shirts. When I got there, the store was not open yet, so I sat on a bench outside until it was. Once it opened, I bought three shirts, headed back toward the car, and realized I did not have the keys. I retraced my steps, checked the bench, and checked the store, but they were nowhere. I called "P," and he calmly suggested I call Pop-A-Lock to make a new key.

While I waited, I went to the food court to grab something to eat. When the locksmith finally came, I walked back to the spot where I had parked, only to find a different car sitting there. I searched the whole lot in a panic, and finally had to admit what I did not want to say out loud. The car was gone. Stolen.

My stomach dropped. Not only was the car missing, but all of my clothes were inside. To make matters worse, it was a brand-new car, still with paper tags. When I told "P," he stayed calm and proactive. He had his mother pick me up, and together we went to get him from work. If he was upset with me, he never showed it. His mother, on the other hand, was furious. Later, I learned she thought I had set him up, calling me bad luck. That cut deep.

Drama, that is how our relationship started. But about a month later, the car was found abandoned, repaired, and returned to him. Looking back, the way "P" handled that moment told me more about his character than anything else could have. He did not lose his cool, did not point fingers, and did not make me feel worse than I already did. He just kept moving forward. That was "P."

By my next visit home, our relationship had shifted quickly from dating to living together. Let me explain.

It was Thanksgiving break, and "P" was on his way to drop me off so I could meet my friends for the trip back to school when my sister called in tears. She told me my son was being mistreated by my mother. This was not the first time I had heard such a thing, and I had even witnessed it myself before, so I believed her. It was already hard enough to attend school so far from him. I called him four times a day just to hear his voice, and that night my heart ached beyond words. I could not leave him again.

Some people may wonder why I left him with my mother at all if I knew what she was capable of. The truth is, Tallahassee was my escape. At first, my son was part of the plan, but navigating a new city with no support was overwhelming. My roommate offered to babysit between classes, but I could not bring myself to burden her with that responsibility. His paternal aunts had said they would take him without hesitation, but my mother convinced me otherwise. I wanted so badly to believe she would take care of her grandson.

That night, I could not follow through with leaving him behind again. "P" encouraged me to go back to school, but I could not risk coming home to a troubled child. I picked up my son from my mother's house and moved straight into "P's" home with him, his mother, and his sister. Looking back, it was wild. I had not even asked or had a conversation about moving in. "P" never said a word, just went with the flow. But the truth is, that decision pushed our relationship to a level we were not ready for. Overnight, he was no longer just my boyfriend; he was a stepfather. From the start, we were already on shaky ground.

As time passed, I realized "P" had been sheltered. He had never been in a fight, had no sense of finances, had grown up without a father, and had little independence. He was a good provider in the sense that if I asked for something, he got it, but I was the one steering our relationship. I had grown up in survival mode, and independence was already part of me. I pulled him along into it, but I was also young and learning myself. Risk-taking was my way forward, and trial and error defined my life.

Eventually, I convinced him we should get our own place. Looking back, it was foolish. We had no credit, he was the only one working, and he made about fifteen dollars an hour, which we thought was plenty. We moved into an apartment with no furniture, sleeping on the floor, while still spending money at the mall and eating out like our priorities did not exist. Some months, we had to take out payday loans just to cover rent, until it became unbearable. We broke the lease and moved right back in with his mother.

In 2012, two years after meeting and a little more than a year into the relationship, we found out we were expecting a baby girl. The reality hit hard—we had nothing to give this child. That season broke us down. Arguments became constant. His mother's house felt overcrowded and unwelcoming. "P" started entertaining his ex, and the whole situation was a recipe for disaster. By the time I was eight months pregnant, our relationship had fallen apart. I moved back in with my mother, and once again, my son had to follow me wherever I went, bearing the weight of all my instability.

I was devastated after our separation. I tried to explain to him that everything we were going through was causing me stress, and that stress was not good for the baby. He didn't seem to care. He stayed distant and would say things like, "I don't want to be in a relationship right now, I need to work on myself." Why now? It felt too late for that. Just as I had feared, I went into premature labor. Our daughter's lungs were underdeveloped, and she had to stay in the NICU for two weeks.

After she was born, we tried to make things work, but it didn't last. When our daughter was three months old, she passed away. Losing her shattered me in a way nothing else had. That grief was different. I felt disconnected from everyone, even surrounded by family, so I ran. Running had always been my pattern when things got too hard. Letting go was easier than facing what hurt.

She passed on December 6, 2012. Before Christmas, I relocated to Georgia. The first three months there, "P" and I had no contact, but his mother remained close. She called often, sent my son and me essentials in the mail, and supported us in any way she could. Eventually, "P" reached out. He apologized for shutting down and even visited me once in Georgia. We tried to rekindle things, but my heart wasn't fully in it.

Life there was hard. My car broke down so often that I eventually had to junk it, every paycheck disappearing into repairs. Without reliable transportation, survival became nearly impossible. I had no family nearby, and as a single mother, I had to teach my five-year-old son how to manage on his own while I worked. Our apartment had almost nothing in it, just a full-size bed, a microwave, and an old box television. I was exhausted, worried about my son, and worn down from struggling. Eventually, I decided the best thing I could do was return home.

"P's" mother and I had been talking about me moving in with her until I could save and get my own place. By then, "P" wasn't living with her anymore. They had fallen out, and he was staying with a friend. A part of me thought the space was good, since I wasn't sure if we were meant to be together. But once I returned to Miami and moved into his mother's home, he came to see me—and he never went back to his friend's house. Just like before, we were pushed back together by circumstance more than by love.

That summer, we spent nearly every day applying for jobs and going to interviews. Finally, I landed a position at a hospital. From the moment I started working, I saved everything I could. Within months, I bought a car and found an apartment within my budget. I had planned to live there alone, but I couldn't shake the guilt of leaving "P" behind.

He wasn't happy where he was, and I didn't want to abandon him. So I invited him to move in with me, too.

We both had new jobs, and for a while it looked like things were finally turning around. The only problem was that deep down, I wasn't sure I wanted the relationship, but I went with the flow anyway. Within three or four months of moving into our new place, everything shifted again. On the very same day I was fired from the hospital, I found out I was pregnant.

At first, I was upset. I didn't feel ready to go through pregnancy again after losing my daughter, but slowly the excitement grew. Around the same time, "P" also lost his job, but we made things work. In many ways, this pregnancy turned out to be one of my best. In 2014, we learned we were having a boy, and I was relieved. I wasn't ready to face raising another daughter, not so soon after our loss.

Those months felt almost peaceful. Every weekend, we went to the movies and out to dinner as a family with my son. I stayed home the entire pregnancy, and my biggest worries were simple ones: deciding what to cook for dinner, keeping the apartment clean, and braving the Miami heat for my son's football games. After the chaos I had endured, I was grateful for that season. Thank you, "P," for giving me a stress-free pregnancy. In November 2014, our son was born healthy and beautiful.

Yet even with a new baby, the cracks in our relationship showed. The biggest source of conflict was my firstborn. "P" provided financially, but there was no personal bond. Watching that distance broke my heart. I wanted my son to have the experience of a present, affectionate father, and he didn't.

Since I am being open and honest, I have to put myself out there, too. In those days, I didn't know how to communicate well. Arguments about my son triggered me, and instead of talking through them, I lashed out physically. I hated drawn-out fights, and when "P" kept pressing an argument, I would hit him. He usually only pushed me away or held me back, but the fights happened in front of my son. That was not okay. I grew up seeing the same kind of behavior, and I carried it forward without realizing the damage it caused. After this relationship, I vowed never to put my hands on a man again. Things could have ended much worse.

One of our most memorable arguments happened one Sunday on the way to church. We stopped at Taco Bell, ordered our food, and sat down to eat. My son was about seven or eight at the time, and he wasn't a fan of tacos. He had his quesadillas, and I encouraged him to try one of mine. I raised it toward his mouth, but before he could take a bite, "P" slapped the taco out of my hand and yelled that I was babying him. I was stunned. I defended myself and my child, raising my voice, and in front of everyone dining in, "P" poured his drink on me. That moment escalated into a food fight, embarrassing for both of us. Needless to say, we never made it to church that day.

Over time, I realized "P" had not grown up in a home where affection was shown. What felt natural for me—hugging my child, nurturing him—looked strange to him. To "P," it seemed like weakness. He often told me I was making my son soft or less manly. His words cut so deeply that eventually, I hardened a little toward my son. I gave fewer hugs and kisses, holding back what I once gave freely. Even worse, "P" made him stop calling me "Mommy." He insisted that it was for little girls, and pushed him to call me "Ma" instead. That broke my heart. I told "P" many times that one day, when he had a son of his own, he would understand exactly how I felt.

Fast forward to 2014. We had a baby boy, and in those early months, it felt like life had settled. But months after giving birth, once the pregnancy hormones leveled out, the feelings I had before came rushing back. I loved "P," but something inside me could not shake the truth that what I felt for him wasn't enough. Eventually, I brought it up in conversation, but neither of us knew what to do with it. We had just had a child together—how could we walk away? I questioned whether we had rushed into things too quickly and were only ever meant to be friends, or if I was simply tired of the constant emotional rollercoaster of trying to teach him how to love my son. Whatever the cause, the reality was clear. Another broken home.

I couldn't hide the truth any longer. I tried to make it work, but my priority had always been my firstborn. I had promised myself he would never feel like I chose a man over him—especially one who struggled to bond with him.

Not long after, we moved from our apartment into low-income housing with "P's" sister. That only complicated things further. Neither of us knew what our relationship was anymore. We both had entertained conversations with other people, and we stayed together mainly because we were financially dependent on each other. The friendship and communication we once had slipped away. He began focusing only on himself and on the son we shared, while I started going out more. Unhappiness hung over us both.

The breaking point came during an argument. In the heat of the moment, "P" asked me which door I wanted my clothes put out of— the front or the back. He told me I needed to be gone by the time he returned from work. My feelings were crushed, but I knew there was no way I could continue living there after that. I called my best friend, and without hesitation, she told me to come stay with her. I packed my clothes as quickly as I could, determined to be gone before he returned. On my way out, I placed his Father's Day gift on the bed, walked away, and never went back.

When he got home, he called to ask where I was. I reminded him of his words earlier that day. He said he had only been playing and asked me to come back, but I was done. That door had closed.

After I left, "P" began operating out of his emotions instead of logic. He became bitter, saying cruel things, sending long messages, posting about me on social media, and making co-parenting difficult. Instead of working together for our son, everything became divided. What I provided was on me, and what he provided was on him. If the baby needed something and I didn't have it, I could not ask him. His motto was, "My son has what he needs when he's with me."

I was too drained to fight back. I let him go through the motions, the anger, and the grief of our relationship ending. I knew his thought process well enough to understand what he was feeling, and I trusted he would come back to himself eventually. Deep down, "P" is a good person, and I believed that would rise again once the sting of our breakup faded.

Still, there came a point where his behavior was too much. The stress of his responses and the constant tension wore me down. Finally, I gathered his personal information and told him I would take him to family court and file for child support. If we couldn't work things out on our own, at least the court could bring order. He didn't want that, so he calmed down. For the first time, we found a little bit of peace.

There were still times when I had to block "P" out, but for the most part, things became manageable. About a year and a half after our breakup, I got engaged to someone I considered my best friend—and someone "P" also knew. That's when the war started all over again. I understood his anger. He probably believed we had been sneaking around behind his back. But the truth is, we hadn't. Things just happened, unexpected and unplanned.

Still, the tension was heavy. I felt like "P" was making my life harder instead of easier, and in my twenty-six-year-old mind, the solution was to move away again. My fiance's parents had offered me the chance to move to Tennessee and start over, and what I wanted more than anything was peace and the space to figure out my life. "P" pushed back, of course. From his perspective, I was taking his only child away. But in my heart, my intentions were never to keep our son from him. I just needed to pull myself out of an environment that felt like it was pulling me backwards.

On the day I left for Tennessee, he had me served with custody papers. Can you believe it? He tried to get full custody of our son. I was furious, but eventually the case was dismissed.

Then, slowly, everything changed. Over the months that followed, "P" did a complete turnaround. Our phone conversations became respectful. He started sending money monthly for our son without me asking. He even traveled to Tennessee to spend weekends with him. On top of that, he sent me gifts for Mother's Day and my birthday. It was like a reset button had been pressed, and we were finally moving in the right direction.

When my marriage began to crumble, "P" stepped up even more. If I needed something for myself, or when I needed him to suddenly take our son, he never asked questions; he just did it. I will never forget one trip when my ex-husband and I visited Miami. Ugly things happened between us, and in that moment, I knew the marriage had to end. I also knew it would be best for my son to stay with his father. Without hesitation, "P" took on the responsibility, and from that day forward, he has carried it with grace.

The roles shifted, and he became the primary parent. To this day, he still is. And he does it with ease. "P" is the true definition of a **FATHER**.

"P" has saved me time and time again. I will always be grateful that God softened his heart and gave him the strength to operate out of love instead of anger or resentment. I know our friendship is a blessing from God. He is someone who genuinely cares about my well-being and has a heart of gold.

When I officially left my ex-husband and moved back to Miami for good, I came with nothing to my name. Without me asking for a thing, "P" saw my situation and took action. He shipped my car from Tennessee to Miami and maintained it after years of neglect. When I found an apartment, he gave me money toward furniture and covered part of the move-in costs. People struggle to understand the nature of our relationship, but when two people are mature, selfless, and committed to treating each other the way they want to be treated, especially when they share a child, it creates space for a healthy bond.

Some people suggest we should get back together because of how close we are, but our minds are far from that. Our only focus is raising our son. We made a decision long ago that no matter what, we would always stand together for him. He will never feel torn between us because what he sees is cohesiveness, love, and peace. And because of that, he gets to live a carefree life, thriving as he grows.

Even in the times when I tried to make my marriage work again, "P" never judged me. He always had my back. In 2023, when my last attempt to save my marriage fell apart, my life was in pieces. I was ashamed to ask for help with rent, but I knew I could lean on him. He sent the money without hesitation. For the first time, he asked if I was okay, and I had to share the terrible truth of what had happened. Still, there was no judgment, only his steady support.

Since then, we have walked a new road together. We've embraced personal development, lifting one another up, learning to frame our thoughts in abundance, and finding ways to create a flourishing life for our son. If my firstborn ever asks him for anything, "P" provides it without hesitation. He and I just understand each other. We add value to each other's lives. We don't argue anymore. We may disagree, but we respect each other enough to talk it through, or sometimes, we don't need to, because respect is already there.

Now it is 2025, and through all the changes in our lives, our friendship has never wavered. It remains steady and true. He is family, **FOREVER.**

Dear "P,"

When I look back over the years, I see so many versions of us—some broken, some hopeful, some learning in real time. And in all of those chapters, you showed up in ways that made a difference. Thank you for who you are, and for who you have grown into. Thank you for taking accountability for the past and for doing the internal work that many people run from. You have always had a good heart; life just had to shape you, the same way it shaped me. Growth didn't come easy for either of us, but you embraced your lessons, and it shows.

I am grateful for your optimism, for the way you speak life into me, for giving me my flowers even on days I felt undeserving. Thank you for your genuineness, for your encouragement, and for reminding me—sometimes more than once—that there is nothing I cannot do.

Thank you for being a steady, devoted father to our son. For guiding him, teaching him, and loving him with intention. For doing the hard work without looking for applause, and for never making me feel inadequate on the days where I'm stretched thin. Your presence has been a blessing I don't take for granted.

Your consistency speaks louder than anything else. Every event, every football game, every milestone—you were there; even for a child who is not biologically yours, you showed up with your whole heart. And that kind of love leaves fingerprints on a child's spirit. Your entire existence has an impact on our son. The confidence. The ease. The way he walks with his head high because he knows he is prioritized and protected. The way he imitates you, studies you, lights up when he's with you. That bond is real, and it is encouraging in ways he may never have to articulate.

You broke a cycle that once broke you. You became the father you needed, the father he deserved. That kind of transformation doesn't just happen—it takes self-reflection, courage, humility, and a willingness to grow beyond your story. And you did that. I see it. I honor it. And a part of me will always hold space for you because of it.

1 Thessalonians 2:11-12 - *"For you know that we dealt with each of you*

as a father deals with his own children, encouraging, comforting, and urging you to live lives worthy of God, who calls you into His kingdom and glory."

With love,
  Star

8

My Angel

Matthew 6:8 - "Your Father knows what you need before you ask him."

My sweet baby girl. I still wonder what she would be like today. I remember the brief time I was blessed to spend with her as if it were yesterday. In September of 2012, I waddled through the baby aisles of Walmart, gathering last-minute items. At 8 months pregnant, I noticed a clear fluid discharge, and that was the day I decided to head straight to the emergency room. My hospital bag was already packed and waiting in the car.

When I arrived, I was admitted immediately and kept for two days while heavily dosed on steroids. The ultrasound revealed that my amniotic sac had a slight leak and my baby's lungs weren't fully developed, so the medical team overloaded me with steroids, so much that I couldn't even keep my eyes open. I remember lying in that hospital bed, eyes closed, trying to communicate with my family through slurred words and half-sleep.

By the second day, September 18, 2012, the doctor first decided to send me home on bed rest, but changed his mind at the last minute and chose to induce labor. Within minutes of the induction, pain erupted through my back and abdomen. In the middle of my anguish, I had my baby's father in a headlock. If I'm honest, I did it on purpose—part of me wanted him to feel the pain he had put me through in other ways. With every contraction, I squeezed tighter. The nurses panicked, warning that I could kill him like that, reminding me that they'd seen fathers pass out under less pressure. But in that moment, I didn't care. I just wanted him to share in my suffering. Lord, forgive me.

The labor was fast. Within 30 minutes, I gave birth to the tiniest little girl, barely over 4 pounds. She was immediately rushed to the NICU because of fluid in her lungs. For two weeks, she remained in the hospital, fighting, before finally being discharged home to us.

As exciting as it was to finally have my daughter home, reality set in quickly—I didn't have much to give her. Still, I refused to let my fears outweigh my responsibilities. I stayed enrolled at Miami Dade College, picked up a job at Macy's, and leaned on her father, family, and friends to watch her while I worked or went to class. I had saved just enough to buy my first car, an old-school Chevy Cavalier from the 1990s, painted in what had to be the ugliest shade of blue ever made, a true bucket, but it got me from point A to point B. The timing was perfect because her father's car had just been repossessed, so I couldn't count on him for transportation to her appointments.

Those months were rough. We weren't together, so the strain of co-parenting made everything feel heavier. I was 21 years old, juggling college, a newborn, and a 5-year-old son. Most days, I felt like I was drowning. My daughter cried constantly, wanted to be in my arms at all times, and rejected everything else, her swing, her car seat, nothing soothed her except me. I breastfed her, which made her neediness even more intense.

One moment that stays with me came when my son looked at me and said, "Mom, I know who's your favorite child." I asked, "Who?"

and he answered, "Aubree." His words cut deep. I burst into tears, overwhelmed with guilt that he even felt that way. I knelt down to his level and tried to explain that his baby sister needed more attention simply because she couldn't do anything for herself yet. I reassured him that my love for him hadn't changed, but still, the weight of his words lingered. Even helping him with his homework became a struggle because the baby wouldn't let me put her down.

What hurt even more was the lack of support from my mother. During my pregnancy, she had seemed excited, constantly asking about the baby, showing concern, and talking about how much she looked forward to her arrival. But after my daughter was born, she rarely stepped in. She could hear the baby screaming from the next room and wouldn't move unless I asked her directly. That contrast, her eagerness before the birth and her absence afterward, confused me and left me feeling even more alone.

As time went on, I noticed something troubling. The baby often made a loud, gasping sound while breathing, as though she was fighting for air. Concerned, I brought it to her pediatrician's attention, but she dismissed me with the words, "She's too young to be diagnosed with asthma." Deep in my heart, I knew something wasn't right, but I didn't know where else to turn. A little motherly advice from my mom would have been helpful, but she barely spent time with the baby and probably never noticed her breathing patterns at all.

Things grew worse. I would be driving and glance in the rear view mirror to check on her, only to find her choking on her milk, silent because she couldn't make a sound. Milk would stream from her nose and mouth at the same time. One night, she was asleep in her bassinet when something startled me awake. I jumped up and rushed over, only to find her choking again, unable to cry, milk spilling from her nose and mouth. That was the last night she slept in that bassinet. From then on, I kept her nose to nose with me in bed, so I could feel her body moving if she wasn't able to cry out for help.

The hardest part was when she went to her father's house. He was a first-time dad, nervous and inexperienced, and he didn't feel comfortable sleeping with her because she was so tiny. I had no control over how he cared for her in his home. All I could do was share what I had witnessed, offer advice, and make suggestions. Co-parenting was a balancing act of fear and trust.

Then came the night that changed everything. I had a long day of school and work, was scheduled to pick her up from her father's house, I was exhausted, and had class early the next morning. I asked if I could pick her up after class instead. In the early hours of December 6, 2012, I received the phone call every mother dreads. Her aunt was on the line, sobbing and panicked. "Aubree's not breathing," she cried. "We called the ambulance, they're coming to get her!" Half-asleep, I couldn't process what I was hearing and asked her to repeat herself. She cried harder: "My mom tried CPR, but she isn't breathing. Blood is coming out of her nose. She's cold."

I flew out of bed and rushed to the hospital, my mind numb. When I arrived, her father and grandmother stood outside the room, silent, offering no explanation. I walked in slowly, heart pounding, and there she was—my baby girl—lying on her back on the hospital bed. Her head tilted slightly to the right, with dried blood near her nose, but she was still so beautiful. I touched her, and she was cold—soft, but stiff. I stroked her tiny curls, and I wept. The grief came crashing down, followed by immediate guilt. I blamed myself. My mind replayed every decision, every choice, every moment I wasn't with her. I fell headfirst into the darkness of guilt.

"I should've picked her up last night. If I had just picked her up, she might still be here."

"I've saved her before, I could've done it again."

"I should've kept fighting for her. I knew something was wrong with her breathing—why didn't I get a second opinion?"

I sat for hours in the chair beside her, staring at her precious face and replaying every moment I had with her. The questions and regrets echoed through me, but I never once questioned God. Deep down, it's like I already knew why she had to leave. As unbearable as the pain was, there was also a strange, quiet sense of relief, and that made me feel guilty. God knew how stressed and overwhelmed I had been. He had heard my cries, my prayers, and my desperate pleas. Psalm 18:6 says, "In my distress I called upon the Lord; to my God I cried for help. From his temple, he heard my voice, and my cry to him reached his ears."

He heard me, and He answered.

I knew He would never put more on me than I could bear, yet the weight was crushing. I felt so alone. It was just me and my Father. During those first days of mourning and every step of my healing, I spoke directly to Him. He knew my thoughts, even the ones I couldn't admit out loud. He knew my fears, my regrets, and the depths of my soul. He was my refuge.

To those around me, I looked calm, almost unshaken. They stared at me with pity, whispering among themselves, wondering how I kept moving, how I could possibly appear so steady in the middle of such loss. What they didn't see were the nights I laid in bed crying until I couldn't breathe, begging God just to quiet the storm in my mind long enough for me to rest. And He did. He gave me peace—the kind that surpasses all understanding. The kind only He can give. Thank you, Father.

Some of you may be wondering what really happened, and to tell the truth, I am still unsure. I didn't learn the full story of her last moments until months later, once her father and I were back on speaking terms. He told me that he fed her that night as usual, expecting her to wake again within a few hours. But instead, he woke up before she did. He noticed she was no longer where he had laid her down. He had placed her at the head of the bed, but she was found at the foot. When he picked her up, she was cold and stiff, with blood running from her nose. Terrified, he ran for his mother, who tried CPR, but it was already too late. His sister called 911, and in a painful twist of irony, my own aunt was the dispatcher who sent the ambulance to their home.

In my heart, I have always believed her lungs played a part. From the beginning, I had heard the way she gasped when she breathed. But of course, the hospital labeled it Sudden Infant Death Syndrome. They didn't want to take the fall. Her doctor knew her lungs were underdeveloped, yet I wasn't sent home with a breathing machine. Afterward, I did my research and realized the medical team had failed us. Later, her father and I tried to seek legal help, but we had no money. The one lawyer who attempted to pursue the case got nowhere because the hospital refused to release documents. Eventually, I gave up. No amount of money could bring her back, and I was weary of reopening the wound. I chose peace, and I chose to let her rest. Recovery.

Losing my daughter weighed heavily on my son, too. He talked about her often, asked innocent questions about death, and wondered how she would have grown through the years. For a year, her ashes remained inside a teddy bear, but eventually, I knew it was time to let her go. One early morning, her father, my son, and I went to the beach. Together, we poured her ashes into our hands. I could feel the tiny bone fragments, both intimate and unsettling. We released her into the waves, and with her ashes, I released my grief. I left the weight of sorrow there in the water, choosing instead to carry love and sweet memories in my heart.

ACCEPTANCE.

Dear Aubree,

My beautiful angel, I often wonder who you would have become—what you would have loved, what would have made you laugh, the little quirks that would have been uniquely yours. You would be almost thirteen now. Time moves on, whether we are ready or not, but I carry you with me every day. I try to keep your memory alive by talking about you with your siblings. They know you existed, but I am not sure they can truly grasp it yet. That's okay. Mommy will never forget you.

I loved breastfeeding you. It was our secret world, a connection I can hardly put into words. You were so attached, so aware, so present. I could not put you down unless you were asleep, and in those moments, I felt the depth of our bond in a way that still stays with me.

I am so sorry, my love, that I didn't fully trust my instincts and seek a second opinion about your health. Sometimes I wonder if you felt pain, or if your little heart knew fear before you left this world. Those thoughts break me, so I try not to linger there too long. But losing you taught me something I will carry forever: to stand firm for what my heart knows is right. I never want to feel that helpless loss again.

You were a child I carried for eight months, nurtured at my breast, a little soul who taught me the true meaning of multitasking, patience, and unconditional love. I wish I could hold you again—hug you, kiss you, rub noses with you, whisper to you. One day, I know I will.

I trust that God cares for you far better than I ever could. He holds you in His hands, surrounds you with peace, and keeps you safe until the day we meet again. My love for you is infinite, eternal, and unshakeable.

2 Corinthians 5:8 - "We are confident, I say, and prefer to be away from the body and at home with the Lord."

With all the love in my heart,
  Mommy

9

Nelly Pooh

Matthew 18:5 - "Whoever receives one such child in my name receives me."

Nelly Pooh. My sweet child. My artist. Unique and set apart from the moment he learned to walk. I remember working the overnight shift at Jackson Memorial Hospital as a patient finance representative. At the end of one shift, I was called into the office and handed a termination notice. The paper claimed I was being let go for sleeping on the job, or something along those lines. Everyone, from nurses to other staff, would take naps during their one-hour break, but I admit there was one time I overslept and returned a few minutes late. I suppose that was what they used against me.

That same night, I kept running back and forth to the restroom, and something didn't feel right. On my way home, I stopped at the store, bought a pregnancy test, and took it right there in the restroom. The result was immediate. I was pregnant and now unemployed. Just wow. But strangely, I wasn't afraid. I wasn't upset. I simply accepted it. The father, "P," had been laid off only a couple of weeks earlier, and while he seemed stressed about our situation, I wasn't. Somehow I knew we'd figure it out. And we did. In fact, this turned out to be one of my best pregnancies ever.

This time around, I was able to stay home, free from the pressure of working for someone else. My days were filled with cooking, cleaning, and binge-watching reality shows. Almost every weekend, we went out to movies, restaurants, the mall, anywhere fun. That was when I discovered Benihana, and I ate there nearly every week. By the third trimester, I had gained nearly 60 pounds. I was 214 pounds, wide as all outdoors, but honestly, the weight didn't bother me until after I gave birth.

The hardest part of this pregnancy was the summer heat mixed with the weight gain. On top of that, I was still a football mom for my oldest son, attending all his Optimist games in the blazing Miami sun. I was miserable, hot, swollen, uncomfortable—but I never missed a game. No matter what, "momma" showed up to support her baby.

Fast forward to the day I gave birth—it still plays vividly in my mind. I went to a doctor's appointment with my mother and a friend. By then, everyone was over it, the doctor was tired of hearing my complaints, and I was just as tired of being pregnant. I climbed onto the office bed, and with his large hands, he physically separated my uterus from the placenta. The pain was unbearable, like fire tearing through me. Afterwards, he told me to get my home ready, pack my hospital bag, and that he would see me at the hospital later that night.

Almost immediately, I began passing fleshy particles and feeling pressure in my lower abdomen and back. The contractions were there, but not crippling yet. I went home, did some last-minute cleaning, packed my son's bag for his grandmother's house, threw a load of laundry in, and finally tried to rest. Even while I was contracting and bleeding, I couldn't just sit still.

Later that evening, I woke up to my cell phone ringing. It was the doctor, confused as to why I hadn't arrived at the hospital yet. "Are you not in labor by now?" he asked. Just as he said it, a sharp pain ripped across my abdomen. "I sure am," I replied, telling him I'd be on my way soon.

But instead of heading straight to the hospital, the father and I decided to walk around the block a few times. I was in pain, but I didn't want to be admitted too early. I wanted to be closer to delivery before going in. By the time my contractions came back-to-back, we finally left for the hospital. On the way, we stopped to pick up my mother. That wait felt like forever. I was doubled over in pain, convinced the baby was coming quickly, while she took her time coming downstairs.

In the car, my mother tried to coach me through breathing exercises, but between the contractions and my frustration with waiting on her, my patience snapped. I was short with her, irritated, and overwhelmed. Sorry, Mommy.

Once we arrived at the emergency room, the staff could see immediately how much pain I was in and rushed me upstairs to labor and delivery. The father stayed behind to find a parking space. When I got to the room, the nurse checked me and said I was 6 centimeters dilated. The pain tore through me, it felt like someone stabbing from the inside, in both my stomach and back. It was a pain I will never forget.

I couldn't stay still. I went from the bed to the toilet, back to the bed, and then I felt the overwhelming urge to push. The nurse barked at me to stop, insisting there was no way I had gone from 6 to 10 centimeters so quickly. I tried to explain that the urge was beyond my control, but she stood on the other side of the room, distracted and argumentative, rather than helping me or calling my doctor.

I kept pushing anyway. Finally, she came closer, and in that exact moment—boom—my water broke all over her face. Inside, I laughed. She had refused to listen, treating me like just another patient, when my body was telling me the truth all along. Many medical professionals get so comfortable in their routines that they forget every woman's body is different. She stood there in shock, jaw nearly on the floor.

Meanwhile, I had literally given birth by myself. My baby lay on the bed crying and cold until I snapped her out of it, demanding she pick him up and pass him to me. By the time his father made it upstairs, after finishing with parking, the baby was already being cleaned by the nurse. The entire labor had happened that fast. The doctor didn't arrive until nearly an hour later.

On November 13, 2014, Karnell Kawhi Smith or as I call him, "Nelly Pooh," was born—healthy, beautiful, weighing 6 pounds and 9 ounces.

As my son grew, I began to notice how different he was. He played with toys, but he also collected the most random little treasures, wrappers from drinking straws, pieces of string, sticks, or bits of nature that caught his eye. My ex-husband and his friends would joke about it, but I always defended him. I saw the beauty in the way his mind worked.

His love for animals, insects, and all of creation was undeniable. When we lived in Tennessee, he would be outside in his water boots from sunrise to sunset, completely entertained by God's handiwork. I often had to yell for him to come inside just before the sun went down. He loved walking to the creek, throwing rocks into the water, and watching Panda, our "borrowed" dog who came with the land and loyally protected us, swim back and forth. He would dig into insect habitats with sticks, watching closely as the bugs scattered, unfazed by bites or stings. He never complained. Those three years in the country were a gift, giving my children the chance to discover themselves and their interests without the world pressing in on them.

It was clear early on that he wasn't drawn to sports. He wasn't even captivated by video games. His world was dinosaurs, nature, and raw materials. Around the age of eight or nine, I noticed his love for drawing. I began searching for art programs and shared them with his dad. At first, his father resisted, he was a sports guy through and through, and he wanted the same for his son. But after trying out track and flag football, it became obvious that sports weren't his thing. He didn't pay attention, had trouble following along, and simply wasn't interested.

Eventually, in 2024, his father discovered an art class, and our son has been attending faithfully every Saturday ever since. His progress has been remarkable. His gift of art is blossoming beautifully, and watching him create fills my heart with pride. I love seeing him thrive in a space that brings him peace, comfort, and just the right kind of challenge.

Sometimes we forget that children aren't meant to fit into society's molds. Instead, it's our job to study them, to see who they really are, to nurture their individual passions, and to place them in environments where their gifts can flourish. When we do that, they can step into their purpose sooner rather than later.

1 Timothy 4:14: "Do not neglect the gift that is in you."

My Nelly Pooh has taught me the true meaning of being yourself. He doesn't bend to what others are doing. He's self-motivated and has the gift of laser focus when he sets his heart on something. I've watched him struggle in math and reading, and I've also watched him fight his way through. At one point, my impatience got the best of me. After long days at work, I'd sit with him, lecturing and pushing, and sometimes my tone brought him to tears. He's sensitive, and I didn't always extend the gentleness he needed in those moments. But instead of staying stuck, he decided to take ownership. Within three months, he raised his F in math to an A, and his D in reading to a B.

That turnaround showed me his determination. It also showed me his maturity, because along with his academics, he began to grow in how he communicated his feelings, his needs, and his wants. Watching that growth has been one of my greatest joys as his mother.

I'm so blessed to have a son like him, a perfect blend of me and his father, rolled into one extraordinary little human being. There is no doubt in my mind that he will go on to do great things.

Dear Nelly Pooh,

From the very beginning, you have loved me out loud. You've never hesitated to wrap your arms around me, lean your head on my shoulder, say sweet words or slip a piece of candy into my hand "just because." When you're out with your dad, you think of me. When you're with me, you think of him. Holidays, random days, quiet moments—you always find a way to remind the people you love that they matter. That is a gift, baby. One of the many reasons my heart smiles because of you.

I've watched you this school year—2024 to 2025—and I've seen something shift in you. Not just growth, but intention. You worked hard. You showed up. You gave your best even when you were tired or distracted or just being a ten-year-old boy who wanted to play. And it reminded me that when a child is surrounded by love, structure, freedom, and parents willing to work together, amazing things start to bloom. You bloomed this year. And I am so proud of you.

Sometimes I look at kids your age who seem so grown, carrying weight they were never meant to hold. But you—thank God—you are still light. Still playful. Still tender. Still a kid. And I pray you get to keep that innocence for as long as possible. The world will try to rush you. Life will try to toughen you too soon. I pray God protects that softness in you.

I know you huff and puff when I make you come to church with me. I hear your sighs, see the slouch in your shoulders, and your little eye roll that you think I don't notice. But I promise you, baby boy, it's not to bother you or make your Sundays boring. I just want you to have something solid to stand on when life gets confusing or loud. One day, you'll understand what it means to build your foundation on something bigger than yourself. For now, just hang in there and trust that Mommy would never lead you anywhere harmful. Everything I do is to help you grow into the man God already sees in you.

I pray you hold tight to your gifts. Your creativity, your sensitivity, your kindness, your leadership. I pray you use them to bless others. When challenges come—and they will—stand your ground. Know that you are never alone. Remember who you are, whose you are, and what God has placed inside you.

I pray I get to see you grow into the fullness of the man you're meant to become. As long as I have breath in my body, I will be by your side—guiding, cheering, correcting, supporting, and covering you in prayer. And even long after I'm gone, those prayers will still be working on your behalf. That's a mother's love—it doesn't disappear. It multiplies.

In Jesus' name, amen.

With all the love in me,
    Mommy

10

Ex-Husband

Exodus 15:26 - "I am the Lord who heals you."

Psalm 147:3 - "He heals the brokenhearted and binds up their wounds."

To be honest, I dread stepping back into this part of my life. I am fighting a lot inside just to sit down and write it. Still, I will be obedient and see this through. We will call my ex-husband "B."

"B" and I met in eighth grade at New Renaissance Middle School in 2004. I had left my previous school because I needed an environment that felt better for learning, and I fell in love with my new school immediately. "B" and Meg, the first girl I befriended, were already close. He would see us eating together at lunch and sometimes join us. I was the new girl, so there was plenty of attention. Not many words at first, mostly looks. If looks could kill, I would have been gone. There were admirers like "B," there were haters, including a group of girls he used to give attention to before I showed up, and there were the customary students who helped me settle in.

One day at lunch, before "B" arrived, Meg told me he had a crush on me and would not stop talking about my beautiful dark skin and my straightened hair with the yellow flower above my ear. My favorite style back then was a wrap with a flower pinned to the side. Yes, I thought I was that girl. After enough convincing from Meg, and after "B" kept showing up kind and consistent—walking me to class, showering me with compliments, finding a way to be wherever I was—I agreed to be his girlfriend.

Things went from zero to one hundred quickly. We stayed on the phone for hours. Between classes, we were always together. He bragged on me constantly. Soon, a lot of the girls decided they did not like me. Not all of them, but most. It did not bother me. They didn't know me, and the only insult they could reach for was my skin tone. By then, I had already embraced my complexion and moved past the stage of feeling small about it.

After a while, all of "B's" affection, the long nights falling asleep on the phone, and the glow of puppy love turned into a mix of distraction and overwhelm. Looking back, I can see how we got there. Let me explain.

On "B's" side, his life was in transition. His parents had divorced and argued often. His mother remarried without telling him and then became a travel nurse, which meant less time together. His father was physically present but emotionally checked out. He never tried to understand football, even though his son had a game every week. He also pushed back on "B" dating me. I was too dark, I had four gold tips on my bottom teeth, and I was from the hood, "Liberty City," as he would say, according to "B," who mimicked his father all the time. My mother was "too ghetto" for him as well. She had tattoos, gold teeth, dated women, and our family did not look traditional. The only person who might have understood "B" was his older brother, but he spent most of his time locked up. Both sons were hurting, but they carried it differently.

I share all of this to give context. I played a major role in "B's" life at that time. I was his first love, his safe place. I encouraged him and helped rebuild his self-esteem. I gave him something to look forward to each day outside the weight of home, and he held on to that feeling for a long time. Literally.

From my side, when I lived in Miramar and could focus on school and "B," I wanted constant communication too. The puppy love was real. But once I moved back to Miami while still attending school in Miramar, my life got crowded. I joined activities, met new people, and soon our worlds did not connect the way they had before. Keeping up with the after-school phone calls became hard, and we drifted. He tried to keep us together, but I had more on my plate than he did.

Eventually, I broke up with him. He did not make it easy, and I was not kind. I was nonchalant, cracked jokes, and handled it poorly. At the time, I felt he would not let go unless I acted out and showed him I did not want the relationship. My god-sister did not help; she encouraged the mess and helped me carry it out.

We tried again at the end of eighth grade, going into high school. We went to prom together. He secretly took me and another girl, which I guess I deserved. We dated at the end of eighth and the start of ninth while I was at Miramar High, but the cycle repeated. I left Miramar, transferred to Booker T. Washington, and we decided to be best friends instead. Really, he settled for the friendship just to stay in my life anyway he could.

This boy was carrying so much at home, and I only added to the load. I still feel empathy for him, even after everything we faced as adults. Stress like that grows into defenses if it is never named or tended. What he needed was healing from his parents. Those needs went unmet, and the pain seeped into his mind and into every relationship that followed.

Over the years, "B" stayed in my life. We didn't talk every day or even every month. Every two or three months, he would call, or he would drive twenty to thirty minutes from Broward into the city to see me. We went to the movies, Santa's Enchanted Forest, or grabbed something to eat. After my first child was born, and after my son's father died, "B" asked to be his godfather. I told him it was a serious commitment, and he said he understood. He came to the christening and stood with us during the ceremony. We were still teenagers, so none of us fully understood what that role required. He babysat once, with help from his girlfriend, and he bought diapers a few times. For a while, his mother gave him a prepaid card for allowance, and he handed it to me so I could buy diapers. I will admit I also bought Victoria Secret's lip gloss, because back then I was obsessed. When my son was about five months old, "B," the baby, and I took pictures at Cute Shots. I can only imagine what his father thought, but I never asked. "B" showed up in the ways he knew how, and I am still grateful for that.

After high school, we went quiet for a while. We reconnected in Tallahassee. He was at Florida A&M, and I was at Tallahassee Community College. I had been there a semester or two before we realized we were in the same city. I lived in off-campus student housing; he had a one-bedroom. By then, his girlfriend was either pregnant or had already given birth to their son. We started hanging out again. He once took me to Walmart to restock my place and criticized nearly everything I put in the cart. As a friend, "B" could be a jerk, saying whatever came to mind and teasing our differences. That is why months would pass between our calls. He also complained a lot about his child's mother. He was so emotional and miserable that I felt bad for him. I began stopping by to cheer him up. We watched movies. His friends would drift in, and we would sit in the living room, talking about high school and laughing at old stories. That summer, I landed a job at a photo place and helped "B" and a couple of his friends get hired, too. We had fun and collected an easy paycheck. I was also taking summer classes, so he let me drive his car to school. I will never forget his old green Acura.

There was a time we drove to Miami and came back to Tallahassee with my son and my little brother, both three years old. Two teenagers, enrolled in school, driving that distance with toddlers in the backseat. Who approved that, and why? The boys stayed with "B" while I went to class. He was no longer in school. He was stressed about his son's mother. They had separated for a bit, and she left him alone in the apartment. If you know him, you know he cannot be alone for two seconds. That is why I stayed to keep him company. Keeping him company turned into living there, but it did not last.

We had a huge argument. I do not remember the details, but I think it was about me talking to another guy. In his mind, we were moving toward a relationship. I did not see how, since he had been asking me to match him with a couple of my dance sisters. My mind was not there. I did not want a relationship with him. The argument sent me back to Miami to finish the summer and figure out my next move. My lease was up, rent had jumped, and I did not want to renew.

After the fallout, we did not speak for more than a year. During that period, I started dating "P." Eventually, "B" moved back to Miami to work things out with his child's mother. When we reconnected, I was pregnant with my angel "Aubree," my second child. We kept a distant friendship, a call here and there, nothing steady. About two years later, he called out of the blue. He seemed better financially, still rocky with his son's mom, and involved in things he should not have been. He offered to buy my son a PlayStation and that is when he initially met "P." At the time, "P" and I were living together and wavering between being a couple and being single. "B" and "P" started doing work together, the kind you have to read between the lines to understand. They did not care for each other, but business was business. After a while, that partnership ended. "P" had realized that "B" was a liar and had flawed character traits. I stayed out of it and let them be.

In 2016, "P" and I finally separated. I moved in with a friend and did not look back. After three months, I found my own apartment. It was in a rough neighborhood, and it was nothing fancy, but it was affordable and it was mine.

Toward the end of that year, "B" and I started hanging out more. We were both fresh from breakups, swapping advice, laughing at old stories, and joking that if our relationships failed, we would marry each other. Did I believe it would ever happen? Not at all. One afternoon, his friend checked my car at a Honda dealership while "B" and I waited at Denny's. As always, he pulled us back to the first days we met. He never lets those memories go. I thanked him for all the ways he had shown up for me over the years. I kissed him, and the rest is history. Star and "B" became a thing. When I told my family, no one was surprised. During our puppy love years, he used to announce that he would marry me one day. I never imagined we would end up together, and I had never told "P" our eighth-grade history. To him, "B" was just my best friend.

The first days were cute, easy, and full of giggles. Then reality set in. How was I going to tell "P"? I knew it would look like we had been sneaking around, which we had not. The weight of it made me question everything. Something in me wanted to back out. The "B" I knew could be loud, unfiltered, and boastful. Back when we were only friends, I would sometimes send him home for doing the most. I ignored his calls for a few days, but he did not let up. He showed up at my job, at my house, and called without stopping. He reminded me of the times he had been there for me. He told me he loved me, that he would do anything for me, that he was not like the men from around my way. My first instinct said no. I pushed past it and convinced myself that it was suppose to be. In truth, I believed what he kept putting into my head. I had no idea what I was walking into. Was it love, obsession, or a bond rooted in old wounds?

It had been thirteen years since we first met, and we believed we had the perfect love story. We went from puppy love to best friends to soulmates. At least that is what "we," no, what he would say. I was pulled into his world right away. His friends became my friends, and his problems became my problems. We lived apart during the week. I was in the city, and he stayed up north. On weekends, we came together. It was laughter, game nights, date nights, and backyard barbecues.

Even then, much of our time was spent with "B" complaining about his ex and all the terrible things she had done to him. I stayed in the circle, offering what felt like a real friendship. His friends and I gave advice, reminded him that he was a good man, and urged him to focus on the good.

His problems were not small. There was the constant conflict with his son's mother. There was the resentment he held toward his parents and the way he spoke to them. Then came the day I learned the FBI had kicked in his door and that prison time was on the horizon. By then, I was so invested that I did not read these as red flags. I saw a friend drowning. I counseled him, encouraged him, and carried him when he could not get out of bed. I became his strength when he was at his weakest. Years later, he would say I stayed because hard living was normal to me. Maybe he thought that. I know I would have shown up for him either way. I still show up with a genuine heart.

Four months before our engagement, we learned he would be federally indicted and would have to serve time. At a restaurant, he broke the news. We cried over the plates in front of us and tried to plan the months ahead. I was crushed. We had been talking about bringing our families under one roof, and suddenly it felt like a dream slipping away. He felt like his world was ending. He needed to get rid of the house, the furniture, the jewelry, and the designer pieces. He was not allowed to see his son. He stayed in bed, depressed and emotional, and most days I was the one speaking life into him. I promised him I would stand beside him no matter what.

March 31, 2017, we went out to dinner with friends and some family. I already knew he would propose. Our worlds did not usually collide like that, so I was able to read in between the lines. I even invited a few people of my own, especially my mother. How was he going to plan an engagement moment for me and not invite my mom? I told her, and she was bothered that he had not called her himself. I did not want him to know I knew, so I sat her at another table to watch from a distance. He stalled long enough for me to start second-guessing it. Then, a little after midnight, April 1, 2017, as we were leaving the restaurant, he dropped to one knee and proposed. I said yes, and in our minds we were swept into a carriage to ride off into happily-ever-after; we were though, minus the horses. Looking back now, he proposed on April Fool's Day. Maybe I should have known better. I'm joking, but it does raise an eyebrow (hope you can hear the smile in that). From that night forward, I was on cloud nine. I wanted to live in his skin.

A few weeks later, near the end of April, he had to turn himself in. That day was heavy. We went to lunch, came home, made love, cried, and then I drove him to the bus station. He took a bus from Miami to Montgomery, Alabama. Once he went through those federal gates, I did not hear from him for a few days. When he finally called, I was at work, and I broke down. The first months without him were brutal. I was depressed, unmotivated, and stayed home. I ate oatmeal for dinner for a month because I did not want to cook. I started to disappear. One day, my mother came over, touched my collarbone, and told me to pull myself together. I looked in the mirror and saw what she saw. From that day, I pushed myself to climb out of that low place.

I changed my view on our situation. The swing from being lifted so high to feeling so low within weeks was more than I could bear. I decided to be optimistic and to visit "B" every month, no matter what. Having a trip on the calendar gave me something to hold on to and kept my spirits up.

Before he left, he added me as an authorized user on his credit cards. He originally wanted to hand all of them to me so I could pay the bills and keep his credit in good standing, but his father advised against it and promised he would handle the payments. He did not. "B" split the cards, giving some to his father and some to me. The ones in my care were paid on time. I made sure at least the minimums were covered every month because that was what made the visits possible.

Twice, I rented a car and drove twelve hours from Miami to Alabama. After that, I got smarter and flew to Atlanta, then drove four more hours. I never missed an email. I even paid extra to get instant notifications so I could respond as soon as he wrote. I sent photos regularly. I did that time with him, fully and without complaint. I believed in what we shared, in what he promised, and in the future I pictured for our family. Things did not turn out the way I hoped, but I trust that God allows what he allows for a reason. There were moments I felt unappreciated, yet I do not regret standing by him. If God had not positioned me there, I don't know if he would have made it through.

Over time, I grew close to his mother over the phone. We started a Bible study together, and she invited the children and me to move to Tennessee with her. She offered help with child care while I worked or returned to school, and she promised to buy a double-wide for us to live in separately. I said yes without hesitation. I wanted to be closer to "B." I wanted another chance to finish school. It felt like a once-in-a-lifetime opportunity.

I was nervous. She lived deep in the country with chickens and a garden, and that part actually excited me. We moved in November 2017, and the culture shock was real. There were very few Black families in town. The nearest store was twenty-five minutes away. The only place hiring was a private prison paying correctional officers thirteen dollars and fifty cents an hour. Everyone seemed to work there, and the only other solid job was at the paper mill. For my Miami people, the paper mill felt like the small-town version of working the Port.

Once the children and I were settled, I started working at the prison almost immediately. I hated it, but it was how I provided for my family. I trained as a correctional officer, lasted one week, then switched to commissary. The pay was lower, but the schedule was better. I had weekends off, I could visit "B," and my mind was at peace. The drive from Tennessee to Alabama was about four and a half hours, and I took my own car. Each month, I brought both children. His son was never allowed to step inside the prison. My kids were young, somewhere between three and ten years old. They did not fully grasp what was happening, but they never complained. They went with the flow and made the best of everything.

"B's" mother introduced us to morning and evening devotions. We sang hymns, read Scripture, talked about what we read, and prayed together. I adopted that rhythm for my home, and the kids enjoyed it. I told "B" by phone and email that I wanted us to do this as a family when he came home, and he agreed. We had no cable, so we used our phones and tablets for Netflix and YouTube, and my son used the Wi-Fi for his PS4. We built a daily routine. We ate healthier. The quiet helped us move through each day with ease. In my heart, I believed that when "B" was released, everything would be better. We would have fun together, pray and study together, and set family traditions our children and grandchildren could follow for generations.

One day, "B" asked if I would marry him while he was incarcerated. I frowned at first. I pictured myself walking down an aisle. I wanted time living together as an engaged couple with him free. I said we should wait to be sure our relationship was sustainable. "B," with his gift of persuasion, told me why now was best. I believed him. My love was real and deep. What could change that?

I obtained the marriage license and ordered our bands on Amazon. He had a black titanium band. I chose a sterling silver cubic zirconia that resembled my engagement ring. On January 21, 2018, in the chaplain's office inside the prison, before my children, his mother, and his stepfather, we said our vows. We looked into each other's eyes, smiling and giggling like kids. It was not my dream wedding, but I was happy to have him as my husband.

Genesis 2:24 - "Therefore a man shall leave his father and his mother and hold fast to his wife, and they shall become one flesh."

Five months later, in June 2018, he was released from prison. I packed new boxer briefs, T-shirts, undershirts, gym shorts, socks, and anything he might need for the halfway house. I drove to pick him up, and it felt surreal. For fifteen months, I could only hug him and sneak kisses during visitation, and now I could have all of him. Our first stop was my hotel, which I had set with rose petals and candles. We could not linger. He had a strict check-in time at the halfway house in Memphis, six hours away. Our hormones were high, we pulled over on the highway to love on each other, and then had to rush to make it to Memphis on time.

In the first weeks at the halfway house, I was allowed only an hour with him. I drove three and a half hours from Olive Hill to Memphis for that single hour. As his supervision eased, he could come home on weekends. We finally slept together as husband and wife. He saw our home and how we had been living while he was away. We woke up to his breakfasts, he practiced recipes because he dreamed of becoming a chef, we played hide-and-seek with the kids, and we rented movies from the local video shop. For a moment, I felt whole. I assumed the kids felt it too.

When his supervision ended, he moved home. Soon after, we learned we were expecting. The baby did not make it. I miscarried and was crushed. From the start, we had talked about growing our family, and not being able to carry our first child together made me feel worthless. A few months later, we tried again, and I miscarried again. Looking back, I feel God was telling me it was not in his plan for us. He knew where our marriage was headed before we did. We can be blinded by desire and miss the signs, which delays what God intends.

Not long after the miscarriages, I felt conflict settle in my heart. With "B" home full-time, things shifted. Our healthy eating faded. He cooked heavy food as he practiced in the kitchen and pushed me to taste things I had given up or never wanted. We argued. He said I was not supportive. He used Scripture to make me feel at fault. Most times, I gave in, sometimes I'd put up a fight, and he would still win.

When it came to daily devotion, he changed the tone until it faded out altogether. We used to start by singing worship, reading scripture, discussing what it meant, and then kneeling to pray. Over time, "B" was not the leader he said he would be. He would not sing. He prayed with his eyes open. He stopped kneeling and stretched out on the couch, saying his back hurt. His body language said he was not interested, and it bothered me. Our scripture talks shifted into lectures aimed at my eldest son, pressure was laid on his shoulders to know it and recite it—without grace, love, or example of how it's done.

We never enjoyed a holiday together without an argument or silence. Suddenly, he did not celebrate holidays at all, though before prison, he did. Who did I marry? I also believe many holidays can distract from what matters, but we could have created our own traditions and taught the children the meaning of family. Instead, everything bent to how he felt that day. Anniversaries, Valentine's Day, Mother's Day, birthdays, holidays—nothing held steady unless he wanted to make a statement. He would buy a necklace, a ring, a bag, but never what I actually wanted. In all those years, he paid for my pedicure once or twice. I had to beg for date nights. My grocery spending was policed. He micromanaged money so tightly that I stopped asking and went without. I decided to go back to work. I could not keep depending on someone who used provision as control.

As much as I hate to admit it, I was low-maintenance and did not ask for much. Instead of appreciating that his wife had a conscience, was understanding, and was willing to grow and learn with him, he took advantage of me. If he had taken time to know me for who I am now, listened to my opinions, and spoken to me with tenderness and genuine love, from a place rooted in today, not eighth grade, things might have been different. I did the bending, the changing, the adjusting, the twisting. It was never enough, and it was never reciprocated. I was told I was the problem. I was too strong. I was like my parents. He was the best thing that ever happened to me. He was the prize. He had done more for me than my own father. Later, when his cooking business took off, the most infamous line: he could buy me.

He began to use things I had confided, deep family and personal matters, against me. That crossed a line. I shut down. He was supposed to be my best friend. My heart lived in a constant ache as the truth surfaced: I may have married the wrong man.

Then things got worse. He says this next piece is what derailed our marriage. From my view, the slide had started long before. There was a man I had talked to before, "B," and I got together. Back when "B" and I were just friends, we shared pasts openly; he told me about women, and I told him about this man. While "B" was in prison, he asked if anyone was trying to talk to me. I told the truth: the man had messaged to say "B" was lucky and he wished he had used his chance better. "B" asked me to block him. I did.

Later, I learned through mutual friends that the man got engaged, so I unblocked him to congratulate him, the same way he had congratulated me. That was it. More time passed. When "B" and I traveled to Miami to host his first dinner sale, the man messaged me asking to buy food. I told "B" immediately. He paused, gave me a hard stare, and told me to have the man text the business phone. I did and moved on.

The next day, driving back to Tennessee, "B" brought it up. Why could the man message me if he was blocked? I had forgotten I ever unblocked him, and it did not feel like a big deal. If it had mattered, I would have blocked him again. I explained. He did not believe me. He was suspicious and hurt, and I could not understand why that one meaningless exchange took so much of his energy.

Another reason I may have seen it differently from "B" is that he was free to talk to his exes on the phone. No one asked if I was comfortable with it. I chose to be secure in what we had and not use his past against him. I judged him by what he showed me in the present. Most of those conversations happened right in front of me, and I was not bothered. When the shoe was on the other foot, he could not tolerate the idea of me speaking to anyone else.

After the first incident, he demanded I never talk to that man again, and I listened—until the man found another way to reach me. Months passed. Then he texted me on WhatsApp, since he was blocked on my phone and social media. The texts were friendly. He asked about the kids and spoke well of his fiance. I mentioned my husband the same way. I told him that any communication was off-limits because of our past. He said he respected that, but every three or four months, he would check in again. I admit I did not block him on WhatsApp, though I never planned to call him.

In August 2019, I came to Miami with the children for my grand-mother's funeral. I asked "B" to come, but he refused, saying it was too expensive. I did not understand why my husband would not stand by me at a time like this, but I swallowed it and kept moving. On my last day in town, hours before my flight, he called to say the man's fiance had accused me of chasing her fiance and always calling him. It was not true, and I felt "B" added extra color to push me into a confession. There was nothing to confess beyond the fact that the man texted every few months, and our exchanges were not inappropriate. Still, I own that I should have ended the contact completely. My husband had set a boundary, and I had left the door cracked.

The timing made everything worse. I was in the same city, and that is when she chose to call him. I had not communicated with the man while in Miami, but optics were against me. "B" told me not to come home because he feared what he might do to me. The children and I had school the next day, so staying away was not an option. I also could not imagine he would ever put his hands on me.

When I got back to Tennessee, it was past midnight. He was awake, and he was angry. We tried to talk, but nothing I said got through. He saw red. From that night forward, the physical abuse began. I knew it was wrong. I knew there was no excuse. Still, I carried a misplaced guilt, whispering to myself that if I had just listened, none of this would be happening. The truth is, we would have arrived here anyway, sooner or later. I was not the first he hurt. I pray I am the last.

What I endured is hard to put into words. I suffered concussions. I was choked until I lost consciousness. I was thrown to the floor and pummeled. The first time I tried to fight back, it only escalated, so after that, I focused on reasoning or escape. He ripped my clothes and blocked the door. Sometimes I sat still, frozen, searching for a way out. His rage gave him the strength of a beast. Once, my younger son called him a monster. That broke me. After each attack, he forced sex. People ask why I did not call the police. He was on probation. I hated what he did to me, but I still loved him, and I did not want to send him back to jail. I am grateful I made it out, and that I found the strength to leave, marriage or not, child or not.

I kept it to myself because I hoped the marriage could be repaired, that the violence would stop. It was not daily. It came every couple of months, sometimes in long stretches, sometimes while I was asleep with no warning. A few times, I know I could have lost my life. Once, on the way to the airport for my birthday trip to Miami, we argued in the car. I tried to fight back because he was driving and I thought I had the advantage. I was wrong. The injuries were not always visible, but I felt them. We boarded the plane, held hands, and pretended.

At dinner with friends, I smiled through a split lip and a pounding head. I could not believe this had become my life. The silence gave me anxiety. I finally confided in my favorite cousin, who was also being abused. We comforted each other, which made the pain bearable but also, in a way, familiar. During that trip, he bought me a diamond necklace or a band, I cannot remember which. I tried to receive it as love, but it reminded me of my parents. My father would hit my mother and then take her shopping. That's what she told me.

I could list every detail of what I endured, but it isn't necessary. That life is over. It's a chapter, not the book. By now, you can see what was, and what wasn't.

During the last incident, I was pregnant with our daughter. In my heart, I knew I couldn't take any more. I called my mother and told her everything. She bought me a ticket to Miami for the following week, timed for when he'd be at work. The problem was getting to the airport; Nashville was two and a half hours away. I called around for a ride, even his brother. His brother told him. He came home early from work claiming he was "sick," snatched my phone, locked himself in the bedroom, and started calling everyone I'd reached out to, trying to poison the well. No one listened.

His business partner happened to be in town and saw everything. I called the police. His mother got involved, not to check on me, but to scold me for embarrassing her in the neighborhood. The officers stayed while I packed. When he realized I was truly leaving, the insults turned to begging. I kept packing. I checked into a hotel on my credit card because he'd emptied our account. He continued calling. I was stunned to be walking out, but my soul was tired.

At the end of June 2020, I boarded the flight to Miami the same day as my twelve-week ultrasound. My oldest came with me; my younger son was already in Miami with his dad. Reality hit hard: I had nothing. We stayed with my mother while I figured it out. He kept calling to "work on us," but I could only see a zeroed-out account and two children who needed to eat. Control was always the point.

God met me in the lack. I applied for food stamps and was approved the next day. I had just gotten my life and annuities license, and it was peak season, so I found remote work, perfect for my growing belly. He hated that I was rebuilding without him and refused to see his part in our separation. The sound of his voice spiked my anxiety. I blocked him for stretches because when he didn't get his way, the nasty side returned.

To this day, I've never received an apology. I've apologized more than once. People say I'm too nice. Maybe. But I refuse to drag old anchors. Forgiveness gives my soul rest. It returns my peace.

Psalm 34:17–18: "The righteous cry out, and the Lord hears them; he delivers them from all their troubles. The Lord is close to the brokenhearted and saves those who are crushed in spirit."

After I left Tennessee, I asked "B" to ship the kids' things I had to leave behind. He refused. I asked him to make the car payment for the vehicle he'd purchased under my USAA account. He refused that too. Thankfully, it was during COVID, and my bank paused the payments. He would not help in any way, but he did suggest I apply for my own credit cards. I did, got approved, and used them carefully—only what I could pay back. Those cards carried me through a lot.

About two months after I moved to Miami, "B" came down as well.

He tried to reconnect. I did not want to. If he loved me, I felt he would have made sure I was okay whether we were together or not, especially since I was carrying his child. I told him that. He didn't get it. Then doors started opening for his catering, and calls and messages from him slowed down.

During my eight month of pregnancy with our daughter, I started having complications. I had been in the hospital for about a week when the doctors decided they needed to take the baby. I called "B." He picked a fight because I had not told him sooner. I had kept quiet because I wanted peace. His presence did not bring that. He drove from West Palm while I was in Miami. By the time he arrived, the baby had been delivered by C-section. He tried to come in, but only one visitor was allowed, and I was drifting in and out from the epidural. My mother handled the logistics because I could not move and kept passing out. I do understand that it wasn't fair for him to drive so far and not be allowed into the hospital, but I truly had no control in that situation. He later used this to say I blocked him from bonding with his daughter.

I wanted to move forward and he didn't know how to. He refused therapy and circled the past, which kept us separated. If I was not with him, he showed little interest in our daughter. The first year and a half sat heavy on me. I had postpartum depression, online classes, and no real help from him—financial or physical. I begged him at times to get his daughter. He said he was busy with work. I reminded him that he set his own schedule and asked him to turn down some events for the sake of his child. He missed her first birthday. He said he was afraid of my family, convinced they hated him. They did not. If I was fine with him being there, they were fine too. He never came to see that for himself.

Every year after she was born, we tried to rekindle things, but nothing lasted longer than three months. The first attempt was awful. He was arrogant, boastful, and acting like God's gift to the world. His rising chef popularity had gone to his head. Women gave him attention, and he said out-of-pocket things I would not tolerate. Whenever I was around him and his friends, something he had vented to them about me would surface. Much of it was untrue. In those moments, I felt foolish to be his wife.

Since Tennessee, we could never fix things privately. He called Tom, Dick, and Harry for marital advice even though none of them were married. He left out his own actions, painted himself as the victim, and collected sympathy instead of wisdom. There was no real change because he would not tell the truth, so the cycle kept spinning.

In 2021, during a custody exchange in a Walmart parking lot, he confronted me about a trip to New Orleans that he had seen through someone's Facebook account because I had him blocked. He asked who I went with, then put his hands around my throat. He squeezed so hard that my necklace pressed into my skin and left a mark. My daughter cried in the back seat from all the commotion. When he realized what he had done, he broke down in tears and begged me to follow him to get food for us. I pretended to follow, turned the opposite way at the corner, and got on the expressway. I drove straight to my best friend's house in case he was behind me. From there, I called the police and filed a report. He called and begged me not to press charges. My best friend urged me to do it. I did not. Maybe it was grace. Maybe it was fear. Maybe it was both.

As time passed, co-parenting with "B" rose and fell. Some days we got it right; other days we did not, but we kept trying. He began spending more time with our daughter, keeping her overnight, sending money when I asked, and we mostly communicated by text.

By late 2022, I was exhausted. I was working, pulled in different directions by the kids, and pushing a divorce forward. I opened the door to marriage counseling with "B" to be sure we had done everything we could. The situation was complicated. He had just moved in with a woman he was dating, and their relationship was already shaky. When I reentered the picture, he treated her differently, and they broke up. That was not part of our plan. We were supposed to try counseling first and then decide. After she told him to leave, I felt obligated to let him stay with me.

She found my number and called. She asked if she should be worried about "B." She said he had hit her in the head with a phone and asked whether she should call the police. I encouraged her to use her own judgment. Soon after, I was helping him move out of her place. Once he moved into my apartment, it got crowded fast. We jumped into the next thing: searching for a rental in Broward, transferring my son to Saint Thomas Aquinas, and draining my savings. I even called my lawyer to close the divorce case. She advised against it. I did not listen.

I still was not sure we were making the right choice, but I promised myself to give it everything. I thought he would do the same. Before the move, I resigned from the Department of Children and Families to complete my full-time, four-and-a-half-month internship for my master's program. "B" was uneasy about me not working. He worried everything would fall on him and later claimed I only got back with him so he would cover my bills.

That was never the truth. I had planned for my internship from the start of the program and built two savings accounts to cover my part. I paid half the moving costs and half the furniture. I paid my car note and insurance five months ahead and set aside my half of the rent for five months. All he would need to handle was his portion of the rent plus food, utilities, and household essentials. I even offered to pick up waitress gigs at my best friend's sister's event space to help with groceries and utilities, but he did not want that. I brought solutions; he brought complaints. Yet when he spoke to family and friends, he told them he was paying for everything on his own.

Not long after we moved into our new place, the problems began.

Some of the things he did just didn't make sense. It was as if he didn't even want to be there. He didn't look happy, and deep down, I felt that he was being spiteful, trying to make my life miserable. I had purchased a truck in my name for him because he had gotten himself deep in debt from buying foreign cars to rent out and was now planning to file for bankruptcy. I didn't feel comfortable buying him such an expensive vehicle, especially a Tahoe, because in the past, he had always taken advantage of me. Still, I tried to stay optimistic and believe that this time would be different.

I found myself trying to meet all his demands. I woke up at 4 AM to get to the gym by 5, returned home by 6:30, made breakfast for the house, packed lunches for everyone, dropped the kids off at school, and still managed to complete my internship hours. What should have felt natural began to drain me. I was exhausted, angry, and confused by how easily he could ask so much of me without lifting a finger to help. I told him he needed to share the morning responsibilities so we could both manage our work and family life. But every year, his view of marriage seemed to change. That year, he decided that a wife should do everything in the home, and if he had to help, he didn't need a wife at all. Hearing that crushed me. I felt used, unappreciated, and unseen. I knew I couldn't live by that kind of thinking.

We began to bump heads more often. My health insurance had run out, so I could no longer afford our marriage counseling sessions. A mutual friend started visiting to help us talk through our issues. Even he could see that "B" was unreasonable and had a strange way of interpreting things. I remember one day he sat with us and helped create a family schedule. "B" complained that I had chosen the same gym day and time he liked to go, claiming I was the reason he hadn't been exercising. That was nonsense. We could have gone together. My son was old enough to watch our daughter, and at 4 AM, the kids were sound asleep. The truth was, he wasn't disciplined enough to wake up early, and I became his excuse.

To keep the peace, I gave up my gym days and took others, even though my favorite kickboxing and boxing classes were held then. Our friend called him out for showing signs of jealousy toward me. I had felt it too, but didn't want to believe it. And did he ever go to the gym after taking my days? Absolutely not.

The arguments grew more intense, and soon the verbal abuse followed. His old ways began to resurface. I warned him repeatedly that if he even balled his fist or acted like he wanted to hit me, I would call the police. One afternoon, he forced me to stay in the room to listen to him. He blocked the doorway and talked for what felt like hours—insulting me, tearing me down, and saying cruel things about who I was as a woman and a wife. Eventually, I broke. I yelled that I couldn't do this anymore, that there was no way he loved me based on how he treated me.

When I tried to leave the room, he pushed and pulled me back each time. My son heard the commotion, came out of the shower, and picked the lock to set me free. That moment still plays in my mind.

"B" always had perfect memory when bills were due, yet I constantly had to remind him to send money for utilities, make the credit card payment, or transfer his part of the rent. He did it on purpose to frustrate me. I told him that since the lease was in both our names and we had a year left, he could stay in the third bedroom. We could continue to handle our responsibilities as adults. But he didn't want that. His only concern was whether I would talk to another man while living under the same roof.

My decision to tell him I didn't want to be with him anymore, along with my suggestion that he sleep in a separate room, set him off. It was April 2023, just a few days after rent was due, and he still hadn't paid his portion. He flat-out refused. He said he wasn't going to pay a dime, that he wasn't leaving, and that I could figure out the rent on my own.

Verbatim he said, "the eviction process will begin." His words infuriated me. Children were involved, and their stability was now at risk. "B" had somewhere else he could go—his parents home, or a friend's place, but my children and I didn't have anywhere else to go.

Out of anger and frustration, I told him that if he didn't send the money, I would let his son's mother know that he was hiding income during their child support case. That triggered him. He called me, threatening to harm me. I warned him not to come home if he was that angry, because I would call the police. His friend arrived at the house first, and then "B" came storming through the front door, charging straight at me. I was on the phone with my best friend and had just taken hot food out of the microwave to feed our daughter. He snatched my phone from my hand, and my friend immediately called the police. The food spilled all over my baby, burning her skin, and she began to scream.

His friend tried to stand between us to stop him from hitting me. "B" clutched my phone, attempting to break it. My son was upstairs, and I yelled for him to call the police. "B" ran up the stairs to stop him. My son was in the bathroom at the time, and "B" burst through the door, invading his privacy and demanding the phone. Panic shot through me. I tried to jump over his friend to get to my son because I feared what might happen next.

When the police arrived, they separated us and began questioning. I explained our history and what had just occurred. "B" lied about his name and claimed he paid for everything in the house, including my phone. He was rude and combative with the officers until they lost patience. Though he didn't hit me, they charged him with interference with a 911 call, resisting arrest, and domestic violence for knocking the food out of my hand.

I agreed to press charges, but all I really wanted was for him to be removed from the house for the night so things could calm down. I couldn't find my phone, and the police insisted they had checked him thoroughly. When my sister tracked my phone's location, it pinged at the police station. I drove there and showed them the evidence. Moments later, they went to the back and returned with my phone. Eventually, I dropped the charges. I didn't want to jeopardize his career or prevent him from providing for his children, even after everything he'd done.

I never received his portion of the rent, even after reaching out to his father for help. Neither of them cared. From that point forward, my finances spiraled. My savings had already been drained from the move, and I was left trying to stay afloat on my own. I signed up for DoorDash, took bottle-girl shifts at an event space, and did whatever honest work I could find to make ends meet. On top of that, I still had to cover my son's private school tuition, which was expensive. "B" had promised to help, but as always, he left me to carry it alone.

Soon, I had no choice but to rely on credit cards to survive. It was a temporary fix that quickly became a trap. I couldn't keep up with the payments while also paying rent and daily expenses. Everything began to collapse financially, and the cards eventually defaulted. Still, I refused to quit. I had only one month left before graduating with my master's degree, and I was determined that all my hard work would not be wasted.

I went to the courthouse and filed for a temporary restraining order. In retaliation, he filed for divorce, knowing I couldn't afford legal fees. I searched online for a lawyer and found one who not only listened to my story but was willing to represent me without payment up front. God made a way, as He always does. When I returned to my job at the Department of Children and Families, I was able to enroll my lawyer in my employer's legal benefits program. From that point on, his work was covered.

Communication between "B" and me was limited to the Talking

Parents app. He was often cruel and condescending, so having a record of our conversations brought peace of mind. At first, his messages would drain me. Every exchange left me tense and emotional, until I learned that not everything deserved a response. I began to answer only when necessary, with grace and calmness. It worked. There was no argument if I refused to join it.

We eventually agreed to a 2-2-5 parenting schedule that gave us 50/50 custody of our daughter. Surprisingly, it worked. He started showing up more, spending real time with her. She adores him, and despite everything, that makes me happy. Every little girl deserves to feel that kind of love from her father. I understand it because I was a girl dad too.

In September of 2024, our divorce was finally finalized. What's crazy is that this was the first day since our separation in April of 2023 that we actually had an amicable conversation. I was caught off guard when he called, speaking for over an hour about everything under the sun, as if nothing had ever happened. I was shocked, but more than that, I was grateful. I thanked God because He had answered my prayer; all I ever wanted was peace between us.

Not long after, he began to call and text more often. Instead of ignoring him, I usually answered, mostly to make sure his mental state was stable. Sometimes he vented about his son's mother, other times he asked for advice or broke down crying about the weight of his own struggles. We talked about the children, about life, about moving forward. And though I once thought I'd be colder toward him, I've realized that I'm not built that way. I forgive easily, I release what hurts, and I hand my battles to God. He fights better than I ever could. Why kick a man when he's already down? That's not weakness, that's growth.

Dear "B,"

I want to start by offering a genuine apology for any hurt or insecurity I may have brought into your life. I know I wasn't perfect, and I know loving me wasn't always easy. Still, I loved you the best way I knew how. I came into marriage without a blueprint, without examples, and a heart still learning itself. So yes—I stumbled. I spoke from wounded places, reacted out of fear, or held things the wrong way. But none of it was ever meant to harm you. I was trying, even though for you, it may have been viewed as not enough.

And even now, with all the distance and all the changes life brought us, I still see the good in you. I've always known you had everything inside you to be a great man and a great father. The only thing that ever stood in your way was the weight you insist on carrying alone. You hold the past so tightly that it spills into your present, shadowing the places where light could come in.

You do not have to walk with that heaviness. You don't have to battle every storm by yourself. There is a God whose power knows no limits and whose love goes deeper than any wound you've ever hidden. Your pain isn't too much for Him. If you were to give Him even a piece of your heart, He would meet you with peace—real peace—the kind that steadies the mind and calms the spirit.

Life has a way of speaking to us, especially in our hardest moments. Sometimes the very chaos we fear is simply a doorway—an invitation to healing, to clarity, to the peace God has been holding for you all this time.

Please know this: I could never hate you. You gave me one of the greatest blessings I will ever receive—our daughter. Thank you for her. She is bright and curious, full of wonder, full of possibility. I see us both in her. And I see you too—your strengths, your softness, even the parts you hide.

I forgive you. Truly. Even without an apology. Even without closure. Forgiveness is the gift I gave myself first, and then you.

Although we cannot return to what we once were, I hope we can build something new—something healthier, calmer, grounded in respect and purpose. A space where our daughter feels safe, supported, and deeply loved by both of her parents. She deserves a world where she grows in peace, where she is corrected with compassion, where she watches us show accountability, healing, and humility. We are both learning. Both unlearning. Both rewriting stories that weren't written with us in mind.

I pray that God softens your heart and clears away anything that isn't reflective of Him. I pray He fills every empty space with His presence, restores your faith, and reminds you of your purpose. May He bless your business, expand your territory, and open doors you never saw coming. And for your son, I pray God's hand guides every step of your custody journey—bringing wisdom, fairness, and a future where he thrives emotionally, mentally, and physically.

In Jesus' name, Amen.

Psalm 103:2-3 - "Bless the Lord, O my soul, and forget not all His benefits: who forgives all your iniquities, who heals all your diseases."

With love,
  Star

11

Princess

Colossians 1:9–10: "And so, from the day we heard, we have not ceased to pray for you, asking that you may be filled with the knowledge of his will in all spiritual wisdom and understanding, so as to walk in a manner worthy of the Lord, fully pleasing to him: bearing fruit in every good work and increasing in the knowledge of God."

My heart, my motivation, my energizer, my daughter, the one who keeps me on my toes, is more than I could have ever asked for or imagined. She entered my life during a season of chaos. The world was reeling from COVID, I was wrestling with abuse and separation from her father, and I was moving from state to state with nothing to my name. Yet even in the middle of that storm, she brought me purpose, laughter, and a deeper revelation of what truly matters in life.

When I first learned I was pregnant with her, I felt both overwhelming joy and piercing fear. I rejoiced at the chance to mother a daughter again, but I worried that I wouldn't be enough, that I wouldn't have enough to give her, given my circumstances. As always, I leaned on God. I prayed daily for Him to silence my doubts and to remind me of

His past faithfulness. With His guidance, I believed I could raise her to become everything He created her to be.

I knew my greatest responsibility would be to teach her the knowledge of God, so that even if I couldn't meet every need, she would always have Him to lean on. And already, at just four years old, she has opened her arms to Him. She prays at night without being told, and she eagerly shares what she learns with her peers. My little princess is a natural-born leader, compassionate, tenderhearted, and unashamed to wear her heart on her sleeve.

Take a trip with me down memory lane, back to before she was even conceived. Well, truthfully, she was thought of, planned, and dreamed about, but here's how it really went.

At the beginning of 2020, my husband at the time and I were already deep in the trenches of a toxic marriage. One day we were good, trying to work things out, and the next day it was World War II. We were as toxic as toxic could be. Before writing this, I revisited some of our old messages from 2018 up until that point, and let me tell you, it was sad. It was unhealthy. It was a season where the last thing we should have been thinking about was bringing a child into this world.

I knew that even then. So when he asked me about having a baby, my first instinct was to say no. Out loud, I told him, "Let's wait until I finish my bachelor's degree." But what I really wanted to say was, "Hell no, I'd be crazy to!" Still, he begged and pleaded. He said he wanted a daughter who looked just like me, and he wanted her name to be Kenya. This was something we had talked about long before marriage, and after enough convincing, I agreed.

Of course, I wanted to have a child with my husband eventually. But in my heart, I knew the timing was wrong. We could not even make it through a full week without falling apart. Yet we convinced ourselves that maybe a baby would fix it, that maybe this child would force us to get it right. As history has proven, it does not work that way.

Well, I was delusional enough to agree to having a baby, and sure enough, all it took was one time for my fertile womb to conceive. I remember hanging upside down off the side of the bed to make sure the baby "made it to its destination," and he even assisted me in doing it. Go ahead and laugh, I know it was foolish, but hey, it worked.

By March of 2020, I learned I was about six weeks pregnant. Happiness and fear collided all at once. I feared another miscarriage, and I feared my marriage would collapse completely, leaving me to raise yet another child alone. We were already on shaky ground. Why is it that human nature knows better but still chooses not to do better? We spend so much energy blaming others or fighting others, but the real war is inside, it is "World War Me." The decisions I made back then were driven by emotions that weren't qualified to guide my life. Those same emotions had failed me time and time again.

Though I've been left to live with the consequences of those choices, I've learned something vital: the only voice qualified to guide my decisions is God's Word. He gives clear instructions and examples of how to flourish in peace, love, and selflessness, and how to experience joy no matter the circumstances. I am listening. I am changing. I am learning to shut out the noise of people's opinions and tune my ear to the whispers of the Holy Spirit. Choices matter.

At the time of my pregnancy, I was deeply invested in fitness, and my body was in its best shape since high school. I promised myself I would maintain that health throughout my pregnancy. While I wasn't surprised by the news, since it was intentional, anxiety constantly pulled at me. I was joyful about the life inside me, but sorrow shadowed the joy. I was recovering from a concussion at the hands of my husband, and the incidents were escalating. Deep down, I knew I could not stay, though I still tried. The marriage spiraled further; less self-control, more abuse, more anxiety, more distance, less love, and eventually physical separation.

Finally, I found the courage to tell my mother what I had been enduring so far from home. She acted immediately, buying plane tickets for me and my son to come to Florida. That very same day, I discovered that the baby I carried was a girl. In truth, I had already been calling her my daughter in my heart.

Once I arrived in Florida, I enrolled in Medicaid, applied for supplemental nutrition assistance, found an obstetrician-gynecologist to care for me during the pregnancy, and began individual therapy sessions. Therapy became a safe place for me to release all that I had been holding inside about my relationship. It felt good to pour out my pain, frustration, sadness, fears, and even my goals. I looked forward to those sessions each week. It was healing to finally speak to someone who did not take sides but simply listened and asked the right questions. Therapy helped me take back control of my mental health. More than that, I knew it was God's grace that sustained me.

Hebrews 4:16 says, "Let us then with confidence draw near to the throne of grace, that we may receive mercy and find grace to help in time of need."

Since I had given birth naturally with my other children, I desired to have a water birth in a comfortable, home-like environment. Because I did not have a home of my own at that time, I chose a birthing center with rooms designed to feel like bedrooms. I have always found that a peaceful environment makes labor less painful and more tolerable. Hospitals, in contrast, are noisy, filled with strangers, and stressful with nurses changing shifts every few hours. That constant rotation of personalities and work ethics only adds to the anxiety of a mother, which in turn affects the baby.

At first, I was excited about the birthing center, but the excitement quickly faded. The father and I constantly went back and forth about who would be allowed in the room during the birth. He did not want to be around my family or friends, yet those were the very people who had supported me and lifted me up during that difficult time. Instead of focusing on me and the baby, he kept turning the conversation back to us, pressuring me about reconciliation. He could not see that true support might have created the very reconnection he wanted. But he was not built that way; it was always his way or the highway.

I blocked him for a while and would sometimes unblock him just to update him on the baby or invite him to an appointment. He never came. At first, he would be calm, but soon enough, he would send the most demeaning messages, which led me to block him again. It may not have been the best way to handle things, but it felt necessary at the time because even the sound of his voice triggered my anxiety.

I tried to silence the negativity for the sake of the baby's growth and development. I thought no communication at all would help, but I learned it only hurt me more. I mourned what I did not get to share with him. I mourned the missed moments: attending doctor visits together, him kissing or talking to my belly, maternity photos as a family, the joy of a baby shower filled with fun and games, and even the simple pleasure of intimacy with my husband. I did not get those experiences. I held it all inside, and the weight of it trickled down to my child and her health. I had to look strong while I was deeply shattered. Shattered, but not broken.

That same November, on the weekend of my son's birthday, we went to Legoland. During the drive there, an intense pressure headache started. By the time we arrived at the resort, my entire body had swelled. My shoes no longer fit. The headache and swelling lasted all weekend, and by the time we returned home, I immediately scheduled an appointment with my doctor. Mild contractions had started, and to my shock, I gained forty pounds almost overnight. This was supposed to be my healthiest pregnancy. I had eaten well, exercised daily, and had only gained a little at each prenatal checkup. Something was terribly wrong.

At my appointment, I was told my blood pressure was dangerously high and was given a 24-hour urinal to fill the following day. I contacted my aunt, who is a labor and delivery nurse, and she urged me to come to the hospital where she worked so her team could evaluate me. After an hour-long ultrasound, the doctors explained that my placenta was calcified and appeared much older than it should have been for me, being only 33 weeks pregnant. The hardened placenta was blocking nutrients from reaching the baby, which left her underweight. On top of that, my pulse was dangerously low, under 2. One nurse even said she did not know how I was still alive.

I remained in the hospital for about a week before they recommended an emergency cesarean section. The nurse grew exhausted from repositioning me all night because each time I lay still, the baby's heartbeat would stop. When the doctors said they had to take her, fear overtook me. I worried this would be a repeat of losing my first daughter, or that this child would suffer from severe complications.

I immediately called the father and my sister so I would not be alone. Since the father lived an hour and a half away, my sister arrived first. She made sure he could still witness the delivery through FaceTime.

Although I was given an epidural, I felt the intense pressure of their tugging and twisting. When they finally pulled her out, it felt like she had been wedged up in my ribs. That is where the pain and pressure were the sharpest. The doctor held her up for me to see, and I cried. She was so tiny, not yet finished baking. Then everything went black.

Hours later, I woke to the most excruciating pain in my stomach where I had been cut. Nausea washed over me as the nurse insisted I go see my daughter in the NICU. I told her I wasn't ready, that I could barely keep my eyes open, but she pushed me in the wheelchair anyway. There she was, my tiny baby girl. Tubes ran down her nose. Her eyes were covered with bands, and a bright light beamed down on her inside the incubator. I tried to keep my eyes open long enough to take her in, but the medication overwhelmed me. With all the strength I had left, I whispered to take me back to my bed.

When I was finally awake and free from the medication, it hit me that I was no longer pregnant. My princess had arrived on November 21, 2020. She weighed only 3 pounds and 4 ounces, yet by the grace of God, she was free of complications. She breathed on her own, she digested her milk, and her only challenge was being underweight. She remained in the NICU for several weeks, and I never missed a beat. I was there every single day, either visiting her or dropping off bottles of breast milk because I refused to let her be fed formula.

Due to COVID restrictions, only one person was allowed to visit her within a 24-hour period, so her father and I alternated days. Just in time for Christmas, she was discharged from the hospital on December 14, 2020, with a breathing monitor to track her heart rate and breathing because of the history of Sudden Infant Death Syndrome in our family.

Her name is Kenya Amira Lee. She carries my middle name, Kenya, but I chose her name with deliberate meaning. While researching, I learned that Kenya has Hebrew roots tied to the word "ken," which means "to horn" or "animal horn." It symbolizes strength, power, and has deep spiritual significance. Kenya embodies leadership and resilience.

Her middle name, Amira, is just as rich in meaning. In Arabic, it translates to "princess" or "commander." In Hebrew, it suggests "words" or "one who speaks, one who is articulate, one who is wise." And if you've ever encountered my daughter, you would know she truly lives up to every part of her name. She is smart, funny, commanding, and magnetic. She teaches, she converses, and she fills every room she enters. My daughter is indeed one who speaks.

Once I was allowed to bring her home, reality hit harder than I expected. Having a newborn who woke every three hours to eat, with no help, was exhausting. There were nights when the alarm on her breathing monitor went off, waking the entire house. Those nights were rough. Her father and I tried to work things out during the first couple of weeks after she came home, but it did not last. He claimed he was too busy with work to help, and soon after, I slipped into postpartum depression.

I never felt disconnected from my child, but I was drained emotionally, physically, and mentally. The lack of sleep wore me down, and all I wanted was a break now and then. My sister stepped in to help with Kenya. She would keep her for me so that I could rest or carve out time for self-care. Thank you, sis.

As Kenya grew, my friend Sam, who was more like my sister, asked to become her godmother. Sam and I had been close since our ninth-grade year of high school. We were different in many ways, yet we clicked. Our bond deepened because my eldest son and her only son were already first cousins, their fathers were brothers, and that connection made our friendship feel even more like family. We were family, through and through, so when she asked, I gladly said yes.

Sam stood before God at Kenya's christening and took her role as godmother seriously. She was more than committed, she was devoted. I never had to ask her to watch Kenya. Instead, she would call and ask if she could pick her up, sometimes keeping her for days or even weeks so that I could rest. Her love for my daughter was genuine and unconditional, and it made me love her even more deeply as both my friend and my sister.

It breaks my heart that Kenya and Sam's relationship did not get to blossom beyond the toddler years. On December 7, 2023, my diary, my sister, and my friend passed away. Even now, when Kenya speaks of her godmother, she says, "She is sick and at the hospital." One day, she asked me if her godmother was ever real. I do all I can to keep her memory alive so that Kenya will not forget her. But I know, as the years pass, time has a way of stealing memories.

Kenya is now four going on fourteen, and she lights up every room she enters. I honestly do not need another daughter because she is about four daughters in one. She is full of life and personality, and she entertains herself with ease. I know she will do great things in life, and I pray that nothing ever steals the natural joy that shines within her.

Kenya is teaching me patience in new ways. I am more mindful now of what she sees, hears, and who she spends time with, because she is a sponge and her memory is sharp. She remembers everything. Her articulation is remarkable, and if she has heard it, you can believe she will repeat it word for word. She loves books, often creating her own stories just by looking at the pictures, since she cannot yet read. She also loves to stay active. Gymnastics is her favorite, and while the other children follow the instructor, she is often off to the side, flipping from the bars and doing her own thing.

She has been blessed with three sets of grandparents, three older brothers, and two parents who have chosen to put aside their differences so that she can have the upbringing we once dreamed of for ourselves. I have no doubt her life will be full, intentional, and purposeful. Kenya is a light that never dims. She does not back down, she makes her thoughts known, she asks her questions boldly, and she listens closely to the answers.

My sons were energetic yet easygoing, less talkative, and not as friendly as she is. But my princess is different. She keeps me on my toes, gives me a run for my money, and even holds me accountable for my own words and actions. You might wonder, how can a four-year-old do that? But her mind is advanced, and she makes connections that surprise me. She recognizes what is right and what is wrong, what should be and what should not. Of course, she still does typical four-year-old things and needs correction or redirection, but even then, she brings me endless joy. She is truly a blessing from God. Thank you, Father, for my child.

Dear Princess,

Right now, you're somewhere in Costa Rica—wild, free, barefoot, and completely at home with the Earth. I can picture you climbing onto your grandpa's shoulders, giving orders like only you can, or curling up next to your grandma as if the world has paused just for the two of you. Maybe you're outside at sunrise, watching the sky stretch itself awake over those mountains, or in the garden pulling weeds with your tiny hands, rescuing little bugs like the gentle soul you are. Whatever you're doing, I know it's with a full heart and a smile that lights up every space you're in. And I'm so grateful God allowed you to experience all of this.

There is nothing I want more for you than true happiness—the kind that isn't tied to things, but to moments. To stillness. To the beauty of God's creation. To the people who love you and the wisdom they carry. That's the kind of wealth I pray your life overflows with.

I want you to always remember this: you are beautiful—inside first, and outside too. You are powerful. Everything you need to succeed is already planted within you. And on the days you forget that or feel unsure, know that you have a village behind you—people ready to lift you, remind you, guide you. And when you can't reach us, or when we are far away, go to God first. He is your source of help, love, peace, and strength. He knows you more deeply than I ever could, and His love for you is even bigger than mine.

As your mother, I will always be your safe place. You can always call on me. I am here for you as long as God allows breath in my body. I look forward to watching you become a young woman—strong, wise, and full of purpose. I can't wait to learn who you become: your passions, your dreams, the way you see the world. I'm ready for our heart-to-heart conversations, for the laughter, the tears, the lessons. I will meet you where you are. I will correct you with love. Teach you with patience. And hold you even when you're struggling to hold yourself.

We will grow through this life together—with open hearts, open arms, and a love that never wavers. I love you so much, Princess.

I pray that you seek God for yourself and fall in love with Him in your own way. I pray your life reflects integrity, strength, compassion, leadership, and wisdom. I pray you remain protected and covered from the crown of your head to the soles of your feet. I pray His grace surrounds you daily and that He spares you from the pain I've known. Take your time growing up. There is no rush. Enjoy the simple joys. Laugh freely. Love deeply. Stay compassionate. Give generously. Pray often. Learn constantly. Help others. Share what you know.

The Bible says in **Proverbs 18:15,**

"An intelligent heart acquires knowledge, and the ear of the wise seeks knowledge."

May that always be your truth.

With all my love,
  Mommy

12

World War Me

Proverbs 3:5-6 - "Trust in the Lord with all your heart and lean not on your own understanding; in all your ways submit to him, and he will make your paths straight."

I have shared different parts of myself with you, and I hope that if you take nothing else away, you grasp the truth that we are nothing without our Lord and Savior. Since the age of fifteen, I have depended on God to carry me through heartache, loss, and disappointment. It has become second nature to lean on him whenever tough situations arise.

But here is the revelation that changed me: I must depend on him in all things, not only in hardship. For too long, I found myself facing the same struggles again and again because I only leaned into God when I was in need. That way of living revealed a dangerous belief, that I did not think I needed him when things were good. I went through life making choices based on what I thought was best for me and what simply felt good in the moment. I did not realize how little I actually knew about life and how deeply I needed him for discernment. He is the one who keeps protecting my blessings, my family, my mind, my peace, and my heart.

God would build me up only for me to revert to my old ways and fall again. That was never his plan for me, but the issue was me. I did not truly understand who he was, who I was, or the purpose for which he created me. April of 2023 was my last fall, and it was the worst of them all. I am still pulling myself out of the hole I dug for myself. When my marriage, my finances, and my home all collapsed, I immediately knew why. It was as if God gave me a clear view of every mistake I had made. I did not even have to ask him why, because the truth was already revealed to my heart.

Even in that season, which by all accounts was the hardest I had ever faced, God did not allow me to hit the ground completely. His grace was sufficient to give me another chance, though not without the consequences of my disobedience. He knew my heart was pure, yet he also knew I had taken matters into my own hands instead of waiting on him. In the midst of turmoil, I found peace and sought refuge in him, and everything about my world began to change. My thinking has been reframed. My self-control, though a daily challenge, has been sharpened. My heart is in constant purification. I am more selfless than I have ever been, and I feel God's presence wherever I go. He has always been there; I just needed to change my environment, my thoughts, my actions, and open my heart to his word so I could finally see him and hear him.

Last year, just two days before Christmas, I heard God's voice clearly for the first time. The sound was mighty, yet calm. A portion of the ceiling opened up, and he instructed me to gather my family, hold a feast, and light seven candles. My heart swelled with love and gratitude. To know that he loved me so deeply that he would let me hear his voice in such a way—it brought me to tears. I immediately began making plans with my family. Though it was difficult to pull everyone together on such short notice, and some tried to back out, I refused to allow it. We came together, lit the candles, prayed, and shared a feast. That moment set a new tone for us, teaching us to become more unified, to show up for one another even when life feels chaotic. There is nothing like time with family. We laugh, we cry, and we love.

Over the years, parts of my life have been displayed on social media, but most people only have a vague idea of what I have gone through. Many know that I lost my son's father, that I lost a child, and that I went through a divorce. They send kind words, telling me how much they admire my strength and my ability to keep going. What they do not know is that I did not do any of it alone. God has always been my anchor. He has provided for me and my children, and he has placed people in a position to support me when I was in need. I have learned that the best way to face hard times is to look for God's hand in everything. When a door closes, I do not see it as punishment or failure, I see it as protection or preparation for something better. That mindset is what has kept me moving forward.

Since 2023, I have carried more than most people could imagine. From the outside, others see me earning a Master's degree, paying for my son to attend an expensive school, and working in a career as a counselor. To them, it looks like I am thriving. What they do not see is the struggle behind the scenes—the times I fought just to put food on the table, the weeks I lived paycheck to paycheck, the bills I had to split in half to survive. My credit, once strong, collapsed under the weight of survival. At the start of my separation, I relied on credit cards until the interest swallowed me whole.

I even had to treat DoorDash as a full-time job, sometimes working more than eight hours a day just to cover $2,700 rent, not including other bills. There were times my children rode with me, because the guilt of leaving them home all day was too heavy to bear. I grew weary, but I never gave up. God was my strength, and time after time, he made a way for my children and me.

During the seasons when God saved me, I would often turn back to my own ways and end up right at square one. Most of the time, I knew when I was doing wrong, but my pride and guilt made me feel too imperfect to bring it to God. I convinced myself that he would not hear me, that there was no point in talking to him, or I would hold off because I was not ready to make the changes that come with true repentance. What I have learned is that Jesus already made the ultimate sacrifice so that I can come to God with all my mess and release it fully to him. I already have access to his power, yet I sometimes let my own mind deceive me. While I condemned myself, God had already forgiven me and was patiently waiting for me to turn the posture of my heart fully toward him.

With the world as it is now, it is easy to forget the promises God has made to his children. Ephesians 3:14–16 reminds me that he will strengthen me when I am weak. Matthew 11:28–30 reminds me that he will give me rest when I am weary. Philippians 4:19 reminds me that he will supply all of my needs when I am lacking. Matthew 7:7 reminds me that he will answer my prayers: if I ask, I will receive; if I knock, the door will be opened; if I seek, I will find. Romans 8:28 reminds me that he will work all things together for the good of those who love him.

Joshua 1:5, 9 reminds me that he will always be with me and never abandon me if I remain strong and courageous. Psalm 91:2 reminds me that he will protect me, even when it feels as though I have gotten the shorter end of the stick. I trust that God has a greater plan and that he sees beyond what my eyes can see.

1 John 1:9 and John 8:36 remind me of his promise of freedom from sin—Jesus has already set me free, as long as I believe it in my heart. Romans 8:38 reminds me that nothing in this world can separate me from his love. When my mind tries to tell me otherwise, I speak life over myself: "He created me in his image, I am worthy of his love." John 3:16 reminds me of his promise of everlasting life. This world has nothing greater to offer than what he has already secured for me, and I believe

that he will do everything he has promised. Unlike man, God never changes. He is the same yesterday, today, and forever.

On my journey of truly grasping who God is and drawing closer to him, I have realized that he is not drawn to perfection, he is drawn to brokenness. I do not believe he wants us to suffer, and I do not believe he only loves us when we are down. I believe our brokenness allows us to receive him as we should. It makes us more moldable, shifting the posture of our hearts so that he can search us, cleanse us of what is leading us to destruction, and make us new and whole.

When I think of the Samaritan woman at the well in John 4, she had been married several times and was living with a man who was not her husband. Yet Jesus met her where she was and chose to reveal himself to her, despite her messy past. She went on to become the first evangelist recorded in the Bible.

When I think of Peter, one of Jesus' disciples, I see his impulsive nature and his tendency to speak before thinking. His faith often wavered. In Matthew 14:22–33, Peter began to sink while walking on the water because of his lack of faith. In John 18:15–27, he denied knowing Christ three times. Yet in all his flaws, Jesus still communed with him.

When I remember King David's fall into sin in 2 Samuel 11, I see a man who committed adultery, impregnated another man's wife, and arranged for that husband's death as a cover-up. And still, in Psalm 51, when David repented, he was forgiven.

I could continue to give examples of God's love, power, and grace, but the truth is that it cannot be measured. Ephesians 3:18 reminds me of this truth: "And I pray that you, being rooted and established in love, may have power, together with all the saints, to grasp how wide and long and high and deep is the love of Christ."

I do not claim to be perfect. I have my struggles, my weaknesses, and a messy past, but through it all, God sees me and takes care of me. He corrects me and guides me in the way I should go, even when I fall short in obedience. I talk to God every day, yet I must admit that I do not always feel like praying. I do not always feel like going to church. I do not always feel like serving others. In those moments, I remind myself that my flesh will always be at war with the Spirit, and I push myself to do the opposite of what I am feeling.

Galatians 5:17 reminds me of this battle: "For the flesh lusts against the Spirit, and the Spirit against the flesh; and these are contrary to one another, so that you do not do the things that you wish."

Choosing to follow Christ instead of the world has not been easy, it is actually the most difficult thing I have ever done in my life. Yet I have discovered that surrounding myself with like-minded believers and immersing myself in a community that loves him makes the journey lighter. There is so much peace in depending on God wholeheartedly. Without question, I know that he has my back and my best interests at heart. That is what it means to walk in faith.

Dear Self,

Look at you. Look at the woman you've become. You have walked through storms that should have broken you, yet somehow—by God's grace—you are still here, still rising, still learning how to breathe again. You're not all the way to the mountaintop yet, but you are far from where you started, and that is something worth pausing for... something worth honoring.

So stay focused on what matters. Keep choosing God in the little moments and the big ones. Let Him shape your vision, your peace, your pace. Life has not always been gentle with you, but even in the hardest chapters, God never let go of your hand. And since He has given you grace over and over again, I pray you give yourself a little of that same grace too.

You are alive, you are growing, and you have three beautiful children who love you in ways that words could never hold fully. They are your joy, your reason, your reminder that God saw fit to fill your life with purpose. So let the world whisper what it wants—about your past, your mistakes, your motherhood. Let them talk. God knows the truth, and He loves you without condition.

Remember there is a calling stitched into your name. A purpose that has followed you through every valley, every lesson, every broken place. Be patient with the process. Let God lead. Use your hands to build, your voice to speak life, and your gifts as a blessing to others. Teach your children the power of the Trinity so they can know God for themselves, not just through you. Their spirits will need Him, just as yours did.

Love your family—those bound to you by blood and those bound to you by heart. Show up with compassion, softness, and honesty. Without love, nothing else stands, because God Himself is love. Keep Him in the center of every plan, every prayer, every new beginning. Let His Word feed you. Let His presence ground you. Let His promises steady you when life feels unsteady.

And hold on to this truth: nothing is too hard for God. Not one thing. He can shift a situation in a blink. Through Him, mountains don't just stand still—they move. Through Him, tables are set in places where you were once counted out.

Be a good steward of all you've been given. Not because you're perfect, but because your heart wants to honor the One who kept you. Stewardship isn't always loud; sometimes it's in the quiet things—the way you care, the way you forgive, the way you choose kindness when bitterness feels easier.

Treat people with the same dignity you ask for. Stand in your truth even when it feels heavy. And remember that every step you've taken—every high, every low—has brought you right here, to this version of you. A woman who is still learning, still growing, still standing strong.

You are doing better than you think. Keep going. Keep believing. Keep trusting the One who carried you through every page of this story.

God's got you—He always has. He always will.

13

Dear God

Dear God,

Thank You for who You are, and for who You have allowed me to become through You. Thank You for loving me past the parts of myself I once hid, for seeing beauty where I only saw brokenness, and for placing grace over the chapters I thought would disqualify me. Thank You for covering me even when I didn't understand the assignment, the pain, or the path. Thank You for the gift of Your Son, and for the freedom, peace, and protection that have followed me because of that sacrifice.

You have been my calm when the world spun wild around me. My strength when I whispered, Lord, I can't do this anymore. My steady hand in seasons that felt like fog. Thank You for being the place where I can lay every burden down, breathe again, and remember who I am in You. When I look back over my life, the valleys, the nights, the storms—I see Your fingerprints on everything. Gratitude rises in me like worship.

It is through You that my eyes opened to truth. Through You that I stood up again when life tried to sit me down. Through You that I speak to mountains and watch them move. Through You that I finally understand that nothing was meant to break me, only shape me. Every chapter, especially the hard ones, belonged to a story You were already writing for my good.

Father, reveal Yourself to me in deeper, softer ways as I grow. Cover my children—my heart walking around in three bodies. Let them discover You for themselves: Your voice, Your protection, Your comfort, Your wisdom. Surround them with favor, shield them from harm, and fill their lives with purpose. Remove anything that is not like You and let Your peace rest heavy on them.

Cover my family—the ones I was born into, the ones life gave me, and the ones whose love has become a home of its own. Cover my friends, the people who have sat with me in silence, laughed with me in joy, and held space for me in sorrow. Bless them. Keep them close to You. Let me be to them what they have been to me: steady, supportive, prayerful, and present. And let love—real love, Your love—guide us all back to You, no matter how far life pulls.

And Lord... the husband You are preparing for me—cover him too. Shape him into a man after Your own heart: steady, gentle, wise, and obedient. Let our connection be rooted in purpose, covered in grace, and aligned with Heaven. May our union reflect Your goodness, and may our lives together serve as a testimony of what happens when two people walk hand in hand with You.

God, thank You. For every door You opened, and every door You closed to save me. For the wounds You healed quietly. For the wisdom that grew from the pain I survived. For the peace that followed surrender. Thank You for turning what once felt like shame into a story that now carries light.

I love You. I trust You. I need You—for every step ahead, for every promise You've spoken, and for every part of this story You're still unfolding.

In Jesus' name,
Amen.

About the Author

Staresha is a school counselor from Miami, Florida, where she devotes her days to nurturing the hearts and minds of children from Pre-K through eighth grade. Her work is guided by compassion and the belief that every child carries a story worth being heard.

Beyond her role in education, she is a single mother of three, a woman who has weathered the storms of love and loss and emerged with a deeper understanding of grace. Her journey has been one of surrender — learning to find peace in uncertainty, strength in vulnerability, and beauty in the places where life once felt broken.

Through her writing, Staresha invites readers into the sacred space of her story — a tapestry woven with faith, forgiveness, and transformation. Her memoir is both a confession and a celebration: a testament to the healing power of God's love and the quiet courage it takes to begin again.

When she isn't writing or counseling, Staresha finds joy in the simple rhythms of motherhood, the stillness of prayer, and the endless pursuit of grace in everyday moments. She hopes that through her words, others will be reminded that even in the valley, God's light still leads the way home.